Philosophy in the Open

Philosophy in the Open

edited by Godfrey Vesey
Professor of Philosophy at The Open University

The Open University Press

The Open University Press

Walton Hall Milton Keynes

First published 1974

Copyright © 1974 The Open University

Designed by the Media Development Group of the Open University.

Printed in Great Britain by
Cox & Wyman Ltd, London, Fakenham and Reading

ISBN 0 335 00909 3

Information on Open University courses may be obtained from the Admissions Office, The Open University, P.O. Box 48, Walton Hall, Milton Keynes, MK7 6AB.

Foreword

We all know what it is to take things philosophically. My favourite description of it is:

> To take what passes in good part
> And keep the hiccups from the heart.

But this book is *not* about taking things philosophically. The philosophers I know do not spend their time brooding on policies for preserving peace of mind in a hazardous and disturbed world. They are as prone to hiccups as anyone else. What they do has little connection with the colloquial meaning of 'philosophical'.

What philosophers do is argue. They argue with anyone who is prepared to argue with them. And they argue about anything from whether fire is hot to whether it is reasonable to expect religious believers to be able to justify their beliefs. This book is a collection of just such arguments.

You do not have to be Socrates or Russell to argue philosophically. Anyone can do it – anyone, that is, with his wits about him and an indefatigable concern for getting at the truth. Philosophy is not a spectator sport. This book is a challenge to you, the reader, to argue philosophically. The challenge is contained in dialogues, discussions, and talks. The six dialogues and four discussions, in particular, positively invite you to participate – either by yourself, or with others (the dialogues were written for dramatic reading). The idea is for you to join in, and take sides. Are you for or against Descartes, Leibniz and Rousseau; for or against Wittgenstein, Parfit and Hare? What do *you* think of their views on the relation of body and mind, predestination, and political liberty; on language and religion, personal identity, and the characterization of moral judgement?

To help you, each dialogue, discussion or talk is preceded by an introduction to the topic under dispute, and followed either by some indication as to how the argument can be developed and continued, or by some suggestions for further reading.

All the dialogues, discussions and talks are part of the Open University's teaching of philosophy. All but one of them – the Russell/Copleston debate – are original Open University materials, broadcast for the first time in the 1970s. This collection of them, with the additional editorial sections, is a prescribed book for Open University students. But the title *Philosophy in the Open* means more than that it is an Open University book: it means that the philosophy in it is open to the intelligent general reader.

G.V.

EDITOR'S ACKNOWLEDGEMENTS

I gratefully acknowledge the kind co-operation of Dr G. H. R. Parkinson, Professor M. Cranston, Professor R. M. Hare, Dr A. Kenny, Mr D. Parfit and the late Professor I. Lakatos, who gave permission for their contributions to be printed in this volume, and of colleagues in the Open University who read and commented on the early drafts of the editorial material.

Grateful acknowledgement is also made to the editors, *The Philosophical Review*, for permission to reprint passages from G. N. A. Vesey, 'Berkeley and Sensations of Heat' in *The Philosophical Review*, Vol. 69, quoted on pp. 18-19; to Elizabeth Anscombe and the Trustees of the Wittgenstein Estate for permission to adapt and reprint passages from Ludwig Wittgenstein, *Philosophical Investigations* and *Zettel*, quoted on pp. 106-12; and to F. C. Copleston, the Literary Executors of Bertrand Russell, and George Allen and Unwin Ltd. for 'The Existence of God' in Bertrand Russell, *Why am I Not a Christian* quoted on pp. 115-20.

Contents

CHAPTER ONE

The World Without

All that I ever learned at college of philosophy had been a conception of the external world as a colourless and soundless wilderness whose true nature one could never know, which one could not even imagine – but which I did, none the less, imagine as a vast landscape of polar spaces in whose eternal twilight one wandered, preoccupied and deluded by a flicker of magic-lantern pictures which danced inside one's mind and for ever remained private to oneself.

Edmund Wilson, *I Thought of Daisy*

THE HEAT-PAIN ARGUMENT

I have the impression that the man in Edmund Wilson's novel, *I Thought of Daisy*, did not like what he had learned at college of philosophy. He preferred another conception of the world, the conception of it as a familiar, warm, colourful, sound-filled place to be shared with others – and perhaps especially with Daisy. I sympathize.

The logical thing to do, however, is not to turn one's back on philosophy in general, but to look for mistakes in the particular philosophy of which the conception of the world as 'external', colourless, and so on, is a part.

What emerges when we do this is that the philosophy in question was originally fashioned to suit scientists. Scientists found themselves able to explain how one event causes another in the physical world without supposing objects in that world to have all the qualities we perceive them as having. Sometimes the scientist and the philosopher were one and the same person. As scientist he adopted a certain method of explaining things; as philosopher he tried to go one step further, he tried to justify his scientific methodology with arguments intended to prove that the things he did not need in his explanations – objective colours, sounds, and so on – did not exist. He tried to prove that colours, sounds, etc., existed only in the perceiver's mind.

The argument that is to be found most frequently in the writings of the philosophers who held this conception does not in fact relate to colours and sounds, though colours and sounds certainly received a good deal of attention. It relates to heat. Perhaps this was because Galileo had claimed of heat that its 'generally accepted notion comes very far from the truth . . . inasmuch as it is supposed to be a true accident, affection, and quality really residing in the thing which we perceive to be heated.'[1]

The problem for the philosophers was: how to *prove* the generally accepted notion to be false.

I think it was the French philosopher René Descartes (1596–1650) who first formulated what I have called 'the heat-pain argument'. He wrote:

> I have a sensation of heat as I approach the fire; but when I approach the same fire too closely, I have a sensation of pain; so there is nothing to convince me that something in the fire resembles heat, any more than the pain; it is just that there must be something in it (whatever this may turn out to be) that produces the sensations of heat or pain.[2]

The British philosopher, John Locke (1632–1704) put the argument like this:

> He that will consider that the same fire that at one distance produces in us the sensation of warmth, does at a nearer approach produce in us the far different sensation of pain, ought to bethink himself what reason he has to say, that his idea of warmth which was produced in him by the fire, is actually in the fire, and his idea of pain which the same fire produced in him the same way is not in the fire.[3]

Another British philosopher, George Berkeley (1685–1753), expounded the argument in a dialogue between two imaginary characters, Hylas and Philonous. Hylas is persuaded to admit that when he puts his hand uncomfortably near the fire he cannot distinguish between the heat he feels, and the pain. It is, he admits, 'one simple uniform sensation'. And being *one* sensation, what is true of the pain must be true of the heat. Like the pain, it 'cannot exist but in a mind perceiving it'.[4]

Hylas, in Berkeley's dialogue, is a born loser. I have written another dialogue, in which I have allowed Hylas to fight back. Philonous, in my dialogue, is much the same as he was in Berkeley's dialogue. But Hylas is a changed character.

I think the man in Edmund Wilson's novel would have liked the new Hylas. They are on the same side.

[1] Burtt (1932) p.75.

[2] Anscombe and Geach (1954) pp. 118–19.

[3] Pringle-Pattison (1924) p. 69.

[4] Warnock (1962) pp. 152–6.

HYLAS FIGHTS BACK

PHILONOUS Good morning, Hylas. I expected you an hour ago, but tell me now, what are the fruits of your further thought? Are you of the same mind as yesterday? Or have you had cause to change your opinion in the meantime?

HYLAS I'm sorry, Philonous, for not meeting you sooner. All this morning my head was so filled with our conversation that I hadn't leisure to think of the time of day, or indeed of anything else.

PHILONOUS In that case I freely forgive you. I am glad you were so intent upon our conversation. Now, if you have found any mistakes in your concessions, or fallacies in my reasonings from them, please let me hear them.

HYLAS To see mistakes and fallacies, Philonous, I would need to have a clearer and more certain grasp of the arguments than I confess I have. Would you bear with me if I rehearse the steps, and you can put me right if I go wrong?

PHILONOUS It shall be my pleasure, though I must admit to some surprise, for yesterday I thought you had achieved a clear vision of the truth that heat cannot exist but in a mind perceiving it.

HYLAS If you would rather that we . . .

PHILONOUS No, no, no. Rehearse the steps. I beg you, do.

HYLAS The argument turned – correct me if I'm wrong – the argument turned on whether or not intense heat is a pain.

PHILONOUS Yes. *You* had said that pain is something distinct from heat, the consequence or effect of it. And *I* . . .

HYLAS And *you* asked me to consider whether, when I put my hand near the fire, I perceive both heat and pain, or but one simple sensation.

PHILONOUS To which you replied . . .

HYLAS To which I replied 'But one simple sensation'.

PHILONOUS Yes.

HYLAS Yes. 'But one simple sensation'. In other words – now this is it, isn't it, Philonous? – my hand feels hot when I hold it near the fire, so very hot that it is painful. And the heat and the pain are one – one simple uniform sensation in my hand.

PHILONOUS Yes. [*Pause*] But, of course, not literally in your hand. Not in your hand, Hylas, as are the bones and sinews.

HYLAS The sensation? No. No, of course not. Though we do *talk* of having sensations in parts of our bodies.

PHILONOUS Indeed, but it is in your hand as part of a being endowed with sense and perception that the pain exists. Were you a senseless being you could not be the subject of pain.

HYLAS That is true. So the pain is in my hand, but only in so far as my hand is part of me, a being endowed with sense and perception. Literally, we might say, the pain is in my mind.

PHILONOUS Exactly. And pain cannot exist in what has no mind. A fire, for example, cannot feel pain, because it is a senseless being.

HYLAS Yes, I quite see that.

PHILONOUS Well then, since you have conceded that when you hold your hand near the fire, the heat and the pain are one and the same sensation, and that the pain cannot exist in a senseless being, you must, to be consistent, grant that the heat cannot exist in a senseless being.

HYLAS Such as the fire?

PHILONOUS Such as the fire. Heat cannot exist but in a mind perceiving it.

HYLAS In other words, the fire itself is not hot. And yet, I tell you Philonous, it is. It is evident to my senses that it is. Can anything be more absurd than to deny it? I reach out my hand to the fire and . . . it's . . . hot.

PHILONOUS [*Stating, not asking*] Your hand.

HYLAS No, the fire.

PHILONOUS But, Hylas, there is only the one simple sensation, and you have conceded that it is one with the pain in your hand. You may, because of it, *infer* there to be something in the fire that *causes* it . . .

HYLAS The heat of the fire I feel by putting my hand near it?

PHILONOUS . . . but, if I may remind you of what you yourself said yesterday, the only things perceived by the senses are those perceived *immediately*. Causes are inferred, and the senses make no inferences. You cannot know, by the senses, anything of the cause you infer to be in the fire; and moreover, it cannot even be *like* the sensation in your hand, for the sensation requires a being endowed with senses and perception for its existence, and the fire is not such a being.

HYLAS So by my own concessions I must be wrong in thinking I feel the heat of the fire.

PHILONOUS Yes.

HYLAS Either I'm wrong or there was a mistake in my concessions?

PHILONOUS Yes.

HYLAS [*After pause*] Hmm. We supposed the heat of the fire to be intense, did we not?

PHILONOUS We did.

HYLAS So intense that my hand feels painfully hot?

PHILONOUS Yes.

HYLAS But suppose the fire to have died down, to be but warm ashes. I touch them, and their temperature is not such as to make me feel hot.

PHILONOUS Is it a pleasurable sensation?

HYLAS Suppose I say it is?

PHILONOUS Well then, since pleasure cannot exist in a senseless being, neither can the warmth you feel.

HYLAS [*After pause*] But when I say it is a pleasurable sensation I mean that I take pleasure in it, just as I do in your conversation. Surely it does not follow from your conversation being pleasurable that it exists only in my mind! And anyway I might feel the warmth of the ashes with complete indifference. [*Pause*] But my point is this. I don't have to feel warm to feel the warmth of the ashes. Rather the opposite. I am more likely to feel warmth if I feel cold.

PHILONOUS Oh, come Hylas!

HYLAS No, I mean it. If my hands feel cold when I put them on the ashes I shall be more, not less, sensible of the warmth. [*Pause*] And you admitted as much, yourself, Philonous, yesterday. Don't you remember? You said that if one of your hands is hot and the other cold, and you put them both in a bowl of tepid water it will seem cold to the hot hand and warm to the cold one.

PHILONOUS I said: if one of my hands *is* hot and the other cold, not if one of my hands *feels* hot and the other cold.

HYLAS All right. But you will admit, won't you, that there is such a thing as one's hands feeling cold? For instance, in the winter, when one has come out without gloves?

PHILONOUS Of course I admit it. If I come out in the winter without gloves, and you shake hands with me, certainly my hands will feel cold to you. But it doesn't follow that the coldness is anywhere else but in our minds.

HYLAS [*Sighs*] No, you haven't seen what I'm getting at.

PHILONOUS [*Slightly irritated*] Well, you said 'There is such a thing as one's hands feeling cold' and I agreed.

HYLAS Yes, but I didn't mean their feeling cold to someone else's touch, or even to your own touch. They . . . simply . . . feel . . . cold.

PHILONOUS Hylas.

HYLAS What, Philonous?

PHILONOUS [*Deliberately*] How is one aware of their coldness if not by touch?

HYLAS That's the whole point. Don't you see? There's a coldness, a bodily sensation, of which one is aware, but not by touch, or by any other means. It's not an objective quality like the coldness of snow, it's simply a feeling.

PHILONOUS But the coldness of snow is simply a feeling. So what is the difference?

HYLAS No, you can't say that.

PHILONOUS What?

HYLAS That the coldness of snow is simply a feeling.

PHILONOUS Why not?

HYLAS Because that is what you, Philonous, are supposed to be arguing for. It'd be begging the question to introduce it as an objection to what I'm saying.

PHILONOUS I'm afraid, Hylas, I'm not at all clear what it is you are saying.

HYLAS I'm saying this. We use words like 'hot' and 'cold' and 'warm' and 'chilly' sometimes to say how *we* feel, and sometimes to say how things feel to us. Sometimes for our 'bodily sensations' and sometimes for the qualities of fire and snow, and so on. [*Pause*] Suppose I say 'My feet feel cold'. I may say this, having touched them. They feel cold to my hand. They would feel cold to your hand. Or I may say it without having touched them. I have a sensation of coldness in my feet. But it – the sensation – isn't something which you, or I for that matter, could feel by touching them.

PHILONOUS Of course not; the sensation is in your mind. It's not literally in your feet. But we've been into all that.

HYLAS Yes, but what I want you to see is that we don't use words like 'cold' and 'hot' *only* to describe how we feel, that is, our bodily sensations. We use them to describe things like snow and fire, and that use is not reducible to the other. When I say snow is cold I don't mean it has feelings of cold-ness. I don't expect it to start shivering or asking for warm clothing. Its coldness is a *quality* it has, not an *experience* it has. When I say that snow is cold and you say that material substances are senseless and therefore cannot be the subject of sensations, we're not disagreeing.

PHILONOUS All right, but it doesn't follow that you're justified in using 'hot' and 'cold' of fire and snow.

HYLAS Why not?

PHILONOUS Well, if I've understood you aright, you hold that there's a sort of dual use of words like 'hot' and 'cold'?

HYLAS [*Agreeing noise*]

PHILONOUS That is, you would say, sometimes we use them to say how we feel, and at other times to describe things like fire and snow.

HYLAS Yes, all right, that's what I'm saying.

PHILONOUS Right. Now, my question to you is this. Given that 'hot' and 'cold' are names of feelings, what justifies us in using them to describe things like fire and snow? Surely if two things are properly called by the same name it must be because they have something in common. They must be like one another in some respect; else why should we call them by the same name? Yet how can anything in a senseless object, like a fire, be like something, a feeling, that can exist only in a being endowed with senses? In the absence of an explanation of that, it seems to me that we have no reason to call a fire hot, or snow cold.

HYLAS We have a reason, namely that the fire feels hot, the snow cold.

PHILONOUS What I meant was that we have no reason to use the *same* words of fire and snow as we use for what you call our bodily sensations.

HYLAS Ah, well now, Philonous, there are two things I want to say about that.

PHILONOUS Go on.

HYLAS First of all, it seems to me that you've put the cart before the horse, if you'll pardon the expression.

PHILONOUS What do you mean?

HYLAS You said: 'Given that "hot" and "cold" are names of feelings, what justifies us in using them to describe things like fire and snow?' But it seems to me that it is our use of them to describe fire and snow that is primary. What is problematic is our use of them to express our feelings. Now this comes out in how a child is taught the words. I can point at snow, and say 'That's cold'. But I can't point at the child's feelings. How a child comes to use words like 'pain' and 'fear' and 'pleasure' as the rest of us do, is the problem, not how it comes to use words like 'white' and 'round' and 'furry'. It's a problem precisely because sensations and feelings are not objective in the way colours and shapes and so on, are. And secondly, I think the explanation of our using a word like 'cold' for a bodily sensation as well as for a property of snow need not be of the kind you describe.

PHILONOUS What do you mean, Hylas?

HYLAS I mean it need not be in terms of our having noticed some resemblance between a bodily sensation and the coldness the snow has.

PHILONOUS But if it comes to us naturally to use the word 'cold' for how we feel, surely . . .

HYLAS Surely there's an explanation? Yes. But the explanation doesn't have to be some supposed resemblance. You said it comes naturally to us to use the word 'cold' for how we feel. Well, the explanation may be equally natural.

PHILONOUS What do you mean?

HYLAS Consider how we use words like 'giddy' and 'dizzy'. They are used to describe someone's state of balance: 'He's unsteady, swaying about'. But they're also used to describe how the person feels. Now, we don't use them in these two ways because we notice a resemblance between a certain feeling and the state of being unbalanced. We call the feeling one of dizziness because it's the feeling that usually goes with being dizzy, that is, being unbalanced. And why should we call it anything else?

PHILONOUS And what about coldness?

HYLAS The same. We call the feeling in our feet one of coldness because it's the feeling that usually goes with their being cold, in the sense in which their being cold is something to be found out by touching them or using a thermometer on them. It's as simple as that. There's no reason why we should use any other word than the one that's ready to hand, that is, the one for the related state of the body. So we use it – naturally.

PHILONOUS All right, but that doesn't show that heat and cold really are *in* things like fire and snow.

HYLAS No, Philonous. But it demolishes one argument for saying they're not, and as far as I can see it's the only argument you've advanced that even seemed like getting anywhere. I know you've got other arguments and I'll be happy to discuss them with you, but perhaps when the sun has gone down. It is so hot.

PHILONOUS You mean it makes you feel hot.

HYLAS No, Philonous, that's not what I mean. The sun *is* hot. Goodbye!

PROOF IN PHILOSOPHY

In Berkeley's own dialogue, Hylas concedes. In mine it is Philonous who finally says 'All right' (though note that it is followed by 'but'). Philosophers in dialogues may be persuaded by their opponents in twenty minutes of fast talk. Philosophers in real life are more resistant to persuasion. Let me illustrate this by relating some of the history of my 'Hylas Fights Back' dialogue.

I had for a long time been trying to find a way of showing the heat-pain argument to be invalid, because I could not accept the conclusion, that heat exists only as a sensation in the mind. I had reached the point of distinguishing between the use of words like 'hot' and 'cold' to say how we feel, and their use to describe things like fire and snow. And I was trying to grasp, in terms of this distinction, the significance of Philonous' insistence, in Berkeley's dialogue, that material things are 'senseless beings'. It struck me that Berkeley's argument must really be as follows:

> We use the same word for a quality of material things as we use for a bodily sensation. We are justified in using it for a quality of material things only if the quality is like the bodily sensation. But they cannot be alike, since one of them requires a sentient being for its existence while the other does not.

17

Therefore we are not justified in using it for a quality of material things.

If I was right in supposing this to be the nub of his argument then a prior question to be considered was: 'Do people in fact suppose themselves to be justified in using the word "hot" of material things, like fires, because they think there is something in the fire like what is in them when they feel hot?' To this the answer seemed to me to be 'No'. And there, for the time being, I stuck, without being able to see how to make any headway. What could explain the dual use of words like 'hot' and 'cold' if not a resemblance in the things of which they were used?

I returned to Berkeley's argument some time later, having in the meantime read Ludwig Wittgenstein's *Blue and Brown Books,* and in particular, his treatment of the question 'What is it that bodily and mental strain have in common?'[1] I tried to apply what Wittgenstein says about the dual use of the word 'strain' to the dual use of the word 'hot', and wrote up my conclusions in a paper entitled 'Berkeley and Sensations of Heat'[2]. In the course of the paper I addressed myself to the question 'Why is it that people unhesitatingly talk of feeling hot as well as of feeling the heat of things?' I wrote:

> There is nothing impossible about a person's forehead feeling cold to him, although, when he touches it, it feels hot to his hand. But this is an exception to the rule. It is the sort of thing which would happen only if the person was in some unusual condition, such as a fever. Usually if a part of the body *is* hot, or *is* cold, it *feels* hot or cold, to the person whose body it is.

> Suppose, however, that there were not this degree of regularity. Suppose, first, that what is true to a limited extent of pain were true to a much greater extent of feelings of hot and cold. What is true of pain is that a bodily feeling which is usually painful may, under certain conditions, be enjoyed. Suppose that, similarly, the effect of a hot bath depended on, say, our emotional state, rather as whether we feel an icicle down our backs as an icicle or as a red-hot dagger depends on what we have been led to expect.

> Usually we would feel warm but sometimes we would feel cold. The closer the number of times we felt cold came to equalling the number of times we felt warm, the more inclined we would be to think of the words 'warm' and 'cold' as applying to the sensation only indirectly. That is, the sensation itself we would apprehend as, perhaps, a mild, diffused prickling, and the warmth and coldness would be our classification of it as 'the sort of sensation which is usually caused by being in hot water' and 'the sort of sensation which is usually caused by being in cold water'.

> If there were no regularity at all, if the sort of sensation which is caused by being in hot water were equally often caused by being in cold water, and vice versa, then

---

[1] Wittgenstein (1958) p. 132.

[2] Vesey (1960).

we would be denied even the possibility of this notional classification. But, as things stand, cases of a person feeling cold when conditions are such as would ordinarily make him feel warm are the exception to the rule.

Now, is it not possible that it is this rule which is the explanation of our referring to the feelings produced in our bodies by prolonged contact with hot or cold objects, as 'hot' and 'cold'? Is it not possible that we apprehend them as feelings of hotness and coldness because the feelings are usually of one sort when our bodies *are* hot, and of another sort when our bodies *are* cold? If this were so, then any inclination we may have to think that the heat we attribute to external objects and the bodily sensation of being hot must be alike derives from our using the same word for a quality of external objects and for a sensation, and not vice versa. That is, we refer to our sensations as 'hot' and 'cold' because they are the sensations which usually go with our bodies being hot or cold; and it is not the case that we call external things hot and cold because we think there is something in common between them and our bodily sensations. So the fact that material things are 'senseless beings', and hence that the heat which is perceived and the bodily sensation cannot be alike, cannot constitute a proof that we are not justified in attributing heat and cold to material things. What justifies us in attributing heat and cold to material things is our perceiving them to be hot and cold; and they could still feel hot and cold to us even if we never felt hot or cold ourselves.

The persuasiveness of Berkeley's argument about heat and pain depends on two things: (i) our readiness to distinguish between feeling heat and feeling hot, and (ii) our having the idea that if two things are called by the same name it must be because we suppose them to be like one another. Only if both these things are accepted can the further point that material things are 'senseless beings' be used to promote the conclusion that we are not justified in attributing heat to material things.

Two years later Professor D. M. Armstrong, in his book *Bodily Sensations*[1], offered an alternative explanation: 'To have a sensation of heat is to feel that a portion of our body is hot.' He described a view he rejected as follows:

> It may be said that a sensation of heat in the hand is not really an impression as of our hand being hot, but is simply something that we normally *happen* to get when our hand heats up. It gets its description 'sensation of heat' simply from the causal conditions of its production.

His objection to this view was:

> On such a view there is a mere *contingent connection* between sensations of heat and the heat of a limb. But if this is so, it is very mysterious that we have no vocabulary to describe the sensations as they are in their own nature, apart from the conditions in which they are normally produced. Their quality seems to be *exhausted*

[1] Armstrong (1962) pp. 39-40.

by the 'conditions of their production', which suggests they are simply *impressions* of heat, etc.

On the face of it, there was an enviable simplicity about Armstrong's own view. And, like mine, it did not lend itself to the sort of conclusion Berkeley wanted to draw, to the effect that we are not justified in calling material things hot and cold. But the more I thought about his view the less happy I became about it. Is not the heat of a material thing essentially something one is aware of by touching it or, if it is very hot, holding one's hand, or some other part of one's body, near it? Yet according to Armstrong one can be aware of the heat of some material things, the parts of one's body, without feeling the heat *with* anything.

In a paper in the *Australasian Journal of Philosophy*[1] I defended the view he rejected by saying that the 'nature' of 'sensations as they are in their own nature' is the nature we apprehend them as having when a certain way of describing them comes to us naturally, and that the reason why a certain way of describing them comes to us naturally need not be a reason of which we are conscious. And I attacked *his* view (that 'to have a sensation of heat is to feel that a portion of our body is hot') by saying that to talk of feeling the heat of one's hand without touching it would be like talking of feeling the roughness of the back of one's hand without touching it.

Armstrong replied, in a later number of the same journal[2], that it is simply an empirical fact about our proprioceptive powers that we are able to perceive the heat of our hand directly but not the roughness of its surface.

This reminded me strongly of Wittgenstein's story of 'the diviner who tells us that when he holds the rod he *feels* that the water is five feet under the ground', and who, when we express our doubts, says: 'You can estimate a length when you see it. Why shouldn't I have a different way of estimating it?'[3] We may say to the diviner: 'You mean, you have learnt that when you have a certain feeling of strain in your hands, then water is usually to be found so many feet under the ground?' But he may reply: 'No, I am able to perceive the depth directly.' Depth being what it is, what can he mean? Similarly, the heat of a material thing being something that we feel *with* some part of our body, what can someone mean who says that he perceives the heat of something directly?

Armstrong's answer to this would, I think, have been that the cases were not similar.

It was with this ten-year-old – and, to my mind, unresolved – dispute at

[1] Vesey (1963).

[2] Armstrong (1963).

[3] Wittgenstein (1958) p. 9.

the back of my mind that I came to write 'Hylas Fights Back'. My primary target was the heat-pain argument, and its conclusion: that heat, like pain, 'cannot exist but in a mind perceiving it'. But I wanted, if possible, to put something into the dialogue that would have a bearing on my dispute with Armstrong about his account of bodily sensations.

I chose the example of our use of words like 'giddy' and 'dizzy'. That someone is unsteady on his feet, off-balance, swaying about, is something to be seen, or, if we are holding him, felt. The person in question may report feelings of giddiness. Is what *he* feels *the same* as what *we* would feel were we holding him?

I think I know how Armstrong's answer to this would begin. It would begin 'No, but . . .'. That is what philosophy is like. As Professor J. N. Findlay once remarked:

> There can be nothing really 'clinching' in philosophy: 'proofs' and 'disproofs' hold only for those who adopt certain premisses, who are willing to follow certain rules of argument, and who use their terms in certain definite ways. And every proof or disproof can be readily evaded, if one questions the truth of its premisses, or the validity of its type of inference, or if one finds new senses in which its terms may be used.[1]

[1] Findlay (1949) p. 352.

CHAPTER TWO

Predestinate Grooves

There was a young man who said 'Damn!
It is borne upon me that I am
An engine which moves
In predestinate grooves
I'm not even a bus, I'm a tram.'

Anon.

CAN WE RECONCILE GOD'S PREORDINATION WITH OUR FREEWILL?

In Part I, Section xxxix, of his *Principles of Philosophy* René Descartes wrote:

> The existence of freedom in our will, and our power in many cases to assent or dissent at our pleasure, is so clear that it must be counted among the first and most axiomatic of our innate notions.[1]

In the next section he wrote:

> Now that we recognize a God, we see that his power is so immeasurable that we hold it impious to believe we can ever do anything but what God has fore-ordained.[2]

His problem was that of how to reconcile God's having foreordained everything we do with our being free to 'assent or dissent at our pleasure'.

That they *can* be reconciled he did not doubt. In a letter to Princess Elizabeth of Bohemia, dated 3rd November, 1645, he wrote: 'The independence which we experience and feel in ourselves, and which suffices to make our actions praiseworthy or blameworthy, is not incompatible with the

[1] Anscombe and Geach (1954) p. 188.

[2] Ibid., p. 189.

dependence of quite another kind which all things share in relation to God.'[1] Princess Elizabeth replied on 30th November, 1645. She could not understand how freewill and preordination could be compatible. Descartes wrote again the following January and attempted to explain the compatibility with a story. There was a king who knew that two gentlemen of his kingdom had a quarrel and would fight a duel if they met, despite his having forbidden duels. He ordered them to go to the same place. They did so, and fought a duel, thus disobeying his prohibition. But even though he planned the whole thing, he did not *compel* them to fight. Their fighting was as voluntary and free as if they had met on another occasion and he had known nothing about it. Similarly, with God:

> Before He sent us into the world He knew exactly what all the inclinations of our will would be; it is He who gave us them, it is He who has disposed all the other things outside us so that such and such objects would present themselves to our senses at such and such times, on the occasion of which he knew that our freewill would determine us to such or such an action; and He so willed, but without using any compulsion. In the King of my story it is possible to distinguish two different types of volition, one according to which he willed that these gentlemen should fight, since he caused them to meet; and the other according to which he willed that they should not, since he forbade duels. In the same way the theologians make a distinction in God's willing: He has an absolute and independent will, according to which He wills all things to come about as they do, and another relative will which concerns the merit and demerit of men according to which He wants them to obey His laws.[2]

That letter was written in 1646. Four years later Descartes died, but the problem of how to reconcile God's preordination with our freewill did not die with him. In the same year as Descartes wrote this letter Gottfried Wilhelm Leibniz (1646–1716) was born. Forty years later Leibniz was corresponding with a Catholic theologian, Antoine Arnauld, about the very same problem.

Leibniz and Arnauld got involved in discussing the problem indirectly – through what seemed to be Arnauld's misunderstanding of Leibniz's notion of 'the concept of an individual substance'. One way of coming to understand this notion is to think of there being any number of possible worlds in each of which there is a near-replica of a person in the actual world. Each near-replica has a life history that corresponds to the life history of the person in the actual world except in just one respect. Now, suppose that one had to make it clear, without using the words 'actual' and 'possible' or their synonyms,

[1] Kenny (1970) p. 185.

[2] Ibid., p. 189.

that a remark was about the person in the actual world and not about any of his near-replicas in possible worlds. The only way to do it would be to give a *complete* description of him, that is, to mention absolutely everything that was true of him. The person in the actual world is the only person who answers to this complete description. Someone who knew this description (he would have to be omniscient) would have what Leibniz calls 'the concept of an individual substance'.

At first glance one might suppose there to be nothing in this either for or against freewill. But it is not hard to imagine someone arguing: If I would not be the person I am, as distinct from near-replicas in possible worlds, unless I do this, that and the other tomorrow and the next day, then what of my freedom to do or not to do these things? Does it not mean that I cannot but do what is contained in the concept of me, that I am, so to speak, *programmed* to do this, that and the other?

This, in fact, is roughly how Arnauld argued.

The dialogue that follows is introduced by its author, Dr G. H. R. Parkinson, Reader in Philosophy at Reading University. It is based mainly on *The Leibniz-Arnauld Correspondence*.

FREEDOM AND FOREKNOWLEDGE

PARKINSON Early in 1686 Leibniz wrote one of his most important works: the *Discourse on Metaphysics*. He sent a summary of the *Discourse* to the Catholic theologian Antoine Arnauld, whom he had met in Paris in the mid 1670s. This summary became the basis of a long correspondence between the two, in the course of which a number of Leibniz's basic doctrines were discussed. From these, I have selected his views about human freedom as the topic of the dialogue which follows. I have based it largely on the correspondence and on the *Discourse*. Leibniz advances these views as an answer to certain problems that spring from his theories about the nature of substance; the main issue, however, is a wider one: whether a man can be *free*, even if all that he does is, or at least can be, foreknown.

ARNAULD I must thank you, Monsieur Leibniz, for the summary of your *Discourse on Metaphysics*, and I am flattered that you think it worth while to seek my opinion. But I am not sure that what I have to say will please you. I will come straight to the point: some of your ideas frighten and shock me. It seems to me that someone who thinks as you do must have a view about man and freedom which no Christian can possibly accept.

LEIBNIZ Just what are these shocking ideas, Monsieur? Be so good as to free me from such dangerous errors.

ARNAULD I have in mind your article 13 – the article in which you talk about the concept of an individual substance.

LEIBNIZ My article 13; ah yes. This is where I say that the individual concept of each person contains, once and for all, everything that will ever happen to him. So one sees in that concept the reasons for the truth of each event; or, one sees why one event has happened rather than another.

ARNAULD Your memory is excellent, Monsieur. But let me point out what follows.

LEIBNIZ One moment, Monsieur; I think I can see what you infer from this. You are going to say something of this sort: that since the concept of the apostle Peter contains the concept of denying his master, then Peter cannot do other than deny Christ.

ARNAULD Yes, that is . . .

LEIBNIZ Consider, now, a proposition about an individual substance. We could choose as an example some particular physical sphere, say, the sphere on Archimedes' tomb, but as my article 13 is about persons, let us take as our example Alexander the Great. The proposition that Alexander died in Babylon is true, and as it is true, the concept of the predicate – dying in Babylon – is included in that of the subject, Alexander. The same holds, no matter what true proposition about Alexander one considers. This is why I say that the individual concept of each person contains all that will ever happen to him. Such a concept I call a 'complete concept'. I distinguish it from the concept of the sphere in general, which is incomplete or abstract and does not suffice to pick out any particular sphere.

ARNAULD I wonder whether everyone would agree with that. A good many would agree that the predicate is included in the subject with regard to the truths of mathematics. Obviously all the radii of a sphere are equal. But they wouldn't be so ready to grant that this holds of individual substances. They would not readily agree, say, that the concept of Adam contains that of eating the apple. They wouldn't agree that eating the apple is part of what we mean by Adam. He would still be Adam even if he didn't eat the apple.

LEIBNIZ But I am sure that when you see what I mean you will see that this consequence does not follow. Let us begin at the beginning; and by the beginning I mean here the nature of truth. You would agree, wouldn't you, that whenever we say something is true or false we are saying something about something? In other words we are predicating something of a subject.

ARNAULD Yes, I agree with that.

LEIBNIZ Now, I maintain that in every true proposition the concept of the predicate is included in that of the subject. Take, for example, the sphere – not any particular sphere, such as the one which Archimedes had placed on his tomb, – but the sphere as mathematicians conceive it. Now, it is true to say that all the points on the circumference of the sphere are equidistant from the centre.

ARNAULD Of course; that is elementary geometry.

LEIBNIZ So we may say that the property of having all the points on its circumference equidistant from the centre is contained in the concept of the sphere.

ARNAULD Yes, I accept that. And if one accepts your theory as applying to propositions like Adam eating the apple then the outcome is fatalism. According to you, the complete concept of Adam embraces all that Adam will do; for example, that he will eat the apple offered by Eve. This means, then, that when God decides to create Adam he is bound to create a being who will eat the apple; how, then, can Adam be called free?

LEIBNIZ Yes, yes, that's just the way I thought you would argue. But I hope to show that you're wrong. I think I can maintain my views about the complete concept of a substance, and be consistent in the belief that man is free, and I hold this belief most firmly. We have to make use of a distinction between two kinds of necessity. One we may call absolute or logical necessity, the other, hypothetical necessity.

ARNAULD I know the distinction, of course – we find it in Aristotle. But I should like to hear how you expound it.

LEIBNIZ To say that a proposition is absolutely necessary is to say that it can't be denied without self-contradiction. If I deny the proposition 'God is God' I obtain the self-contradiction 'God is not God'; so the proposition 'God is God' is absolutely necessary. On the other hand, to say that a proposition is hypothetically necessary is to say that there is *no* self-contradiction in denying it. . . .

ARNAULD But if there's no self-contradiction in denying something then surely it is *not necessary*. Why then do you call it necessary – or rather hypothetically necessary? Where does the hypothesis come in?

LEIBNIZ In this way. If God decided to create the particular Adam who ate the apple – then it would be necessary that Adam ate it. The word 'hypothesis' refers to the supposition that God decided to create that particular Adam. We are speaking here of what is necessary given that something else is the case.

ARNAULD Very well. I see what you mean. But if God decides to actualize the concept of an Adam who eats the apple, then surely Adam must eat the apple. That is my point. You are still denying that man is free. [*Pause*] But I think I can help you with a way out of the difficulty. I agree that, if God decides to create a man called Antoine Arnauld, then he must create a being who is capable of thought. But it was by no means necessary for God to create an Arnauld who is a bachelor; for I should remain myself whether I were married or not. I propose to say, then, that there belongs to the individual concept of myself everything which is such that, in its absence, I should no longer be me. For example, thought belongs to my individual concept, but being a bachelor does not; and therefore I was free to marry or not.

LEIBNIZ I can't agree with that. Perhaps I may persuade you to accept *my* point of view if I relate what we have been saying to certain problems of theology.

ARNAULD That may help; and indeed I could wish [*dry chuckle*] that you would abandon these metaphysical speculations and apply yourself to the business of your salvation.

LEIBNIZ You agree, do you not, that God is the creator of everything, and therefore is the creator of Arnauld?

ARNAULD Of course I do.

LEIBNIZ You agree also, I imagine, that God knows everything – not only what happens and has happened, but also what will happen?

ARNAULD Certainly.

LEIBNIZ It follows, then, that before God decides to create Arnauld, he knows all that Arnauld will do. From this there arise difficulties which, I am sure, are familiar to you – difficulties about God's foreknowledge and his pre-ordination. Since God foreknows what Arnauld will do, how can Arnauld be free to do it or not to do it? Since God has created an Arnauld who will be a bachelor, how can Arnauld be anything other than a bachelor? These are familiar difficulties, as I say; I mention them because they are related to my views about the complete concept of a substance. A theologian will say that God foreknows that Arnauld will be a bachelor; I say that the complete concept of Arnauld (which God has) includes his being a bachelor. A theologian will say that what you are is preordained by God; I say that God has decided to actualize a complete concept which includes your decision not to marry. Now, one *cannot* escape this difficulty as you propose by saying that the complete concept of Arnauld does *not* include his being a bachelor; this would amount to saying that God is not all-knowing.

ARNAULD I see now in what sense my individual concept includes my being a bachelor. But whereas the definition I gave of an individual concept enables us to draw a distinction between my being a rational creature and being a bachelor, I can't see that *your* definition allows this. From what you say, it seems that I cannot *but* be a bachelor. But I chose not to marry and we both agree that this was a free choice; the question is whether this freedom is consistent with your principles. But now, let us ask another question: just what constitutes the freedom of this choice? To say that my choice is free is surely to say that it is undetermined; but in what sense can this be said?

LEIBNIZ One thing is certain: one's freedom of choice does not consist in an absence of reasons for one's choice. As I see it, to be free is to have the power to do otherwise, or to suspend one's action altogether; to be free is for an alternative to one's action to be possible. But freedom does not consist in acting without reason. As you say, your decision not to marry was a free one, but it was not without its reasons: you wished to enter into the service of God. Everything has a reason in my view. Every true proposition can be proved; in other words a reason for its truth can always be given.

ARNAULD One moment: I see a difficulty here. If everything has a reason, how are we to distinguish between the fact that Arnauld is a rational being, and the fact that Arnauld is a bachelor? Is there a difference in the way the reasons operate?

LEIBNIZ I was just about to explain this. In the case of a choice, which is what concerns us here, the reasons merely incline – they do not necessitate.

ARNAULD I noted this phrase in the summary of your discourse, Monsieur, and I must say it leaves me somewhat puzzled. It reminds me of what some of the Scholastics have said, 'The stars incline, they do not necessitate.'

LEIBNIZ I had that saying in mind.

ARNAULD But the philosophers who said this meant that although the stars have some influence on us, they do not influence completely what we do.

Do you mean, then, that when I act from a certain motive, that motive does not determine my action completely? From what you have just been saying, this seems unlikely.

LEIBNIZ I don't mean this. Let me try to explain what I do mean. When we act from a certain motive, or from the strongest one when there has been a conflict between motives, then there is a sense in which we must act as we do.

ARNAULD But . . .

LEIBNIZ Allow me, Monsieur. As I explain in my discourse, God has so created us that our will always tends towards the apparent good – to what we think to be good, whether or not it really is good. In other words, God determines our will to choose what seems good, or seems the best. But God does not necessitate our will. Although we always follow the strongest motive, some other choice is always logically possible; and this is why I say that the reasons for a choice incline, but do not necessitate.

ARNAULD Logically possible? But surely there is more to freedom than a logical possibility.

LEIBNIZ No: Adam sins as he does because otherwise he would not be Adam; the concept that God has of him contains this free action, and God decides to actualize this concept.

ARNAULD If you say this, must you not . . .?

LEIBNIZ But I would like to add one thing. Someone may try to use what I have been saying to shift the blame for sin from the sinner to God.

ARNAULD Yes, that was in my mind. And this is why I said earlier that no Christian can possibly accept your view of man. I can imagine someone arguing like this. 'You say that Adam sins as he does because otherwise he would not be Adam. Very well: but this Adam, this Adam who eats the apple, has been created because God decides that there shall be an Adam who eats the apple. It is all, one might say, part of God's plan. How, then, can Adam be blamed for what he does?'

LEIBNIZ Such a use of my views would be quite wrong. Consider Adam just before his sin. He is free to do what he wants to do; what more can he ask? Can he rightly complain that God has determined him to eat the apple? Surely not; what God has decided in such matters cannot be known before the event by mere finite beings like ourselves. Adam cannot know that God has determined him to sin, unless he is already sinning.

ARNAULD But might not Adam have said to himself, 'Perhaps it has been determined from all eternity, that I shall sin'?

LEIBNIZ He might indeed: but then he should have added, 'Perhaps it has not'. And we should say just the same. We should not worry about what we cannot know; we should not try to plumb the depths of the divine wisdom. We should try to act in accordance with our duty, which we do know.

ARNAULD I heartily agree with that, Monsieur; and your duty is to look to your salvation.

SELF-DETERMINISM

In the dialogue Arnauld asks 'To say that my choice is free is surely to say that it is undetermined; but in what sense can this be said?'

Descartes would have answered: In the sense that I am not *compelled* to choose as I do. The choice is determined by the inclinations of my own will, not imposed on me against my will. The fact that God gave me the inclinations of my will is beside the point.

Leibniz would agree with this. In the dialogue he says: 'Consider Adam just before his sin. He is free to do what he wants to do. What more can he ask?'

But Leibniz does not stop there. He adds:

Can [Adam] rightly complain that God has determined him to eat the apple? Surely not; what God has decided in such matters cannot be known before the event by mere finite beings like ourselves.

This suggests that Leibniz thinks freedom should be understood not in terms of *not being* determined but in terms of being determined but *not knowing* what one is determined to do. Finite beings like ourselves cannot know before the event what God has determined us to do; hence we are free.

Put like this, it is not very plausible as an account of what we mean by 'free'. We do not want our much-vaunted freedom to be a matter of what we happen not to know. And yet there does seem to be a connection of some sort between freedom and ignorance, even if we have not got it quite right. Have we gone wrong in trying to describe it in terms of what we *happen* not to know? Is it, rather, a connection between freedom and what we *cannot* know?

Consideration of this question is complicated by our thinking of our actions as being determined by God. Let us remove the question from this theological context. Let us merely suppose that to any choice of action I make there corresponds a physical change in my brain, and that physical changes in the brain are wholly determined by prior physical changes in the brain. Would it follow that I could be told, by a super-physiologist who had been observing my brain-workings, what I was bound to decide to do in a moment's time?

A negative answer to this question has been given, and argued for, in a paper 'Brain and Will' by D. M. MacKay, Professor of Communication at the University of Keele. MacKay rejects the view that we can be held to be free only if processes in the brain are not physically determinate. He writes:

> I believe that whether the brain-mechanism is physically determinate or not, the activity which we call 'making a free choice' is of a special kind which could never be described to us with certainty beforehand. Suppose we are asked to choose between porridge and prunes for breakfast. We think: 'Let's see: I've had prunes all last week; I'm sick of prunes; I'll have porridge.' We would normally claim now to have made a 'free choice'. But suppose that some super-physiologist has been observing our brain-workings all this time, and suppose he declares that our brain went through nothing but physically determinate actions. Does this mean that he could have told us in advance that we would certainly choose porridge? Of course not. However carefully calculated his proffered description of our choice, we would know – and he would know – that we still had power to alter it.
>
> No matter how much he tried to allow in advance for the effects of his telling us, we could still defy him to give us a guaranteed description of what our choice would be. This is our plain everyday experience of what most people mean by a free choice: a choice which nobody could (even in principle) describe to us with certainty in advance. My point is that this vital criterion of freedom of choice, which we shall see later can be extended and strengthened, would apply equally well whether the brain were physically determinate in its workings or not. In either case, the state of our brain after receiving his description would not (and could not) be the state on which he based his calculations. If he were to try to allow beforehand for the effects of his description upon us, he would be doomed to an endless regression – logically chasing his own tail in an effort to allow for the effects of allowing for the effects of allowing . . . indefinitely.[1]

I think it very unlikely that most people, if they were asked what they meant by 'a free choice' would give the same answer, let alone the answer 'a choice which nobody could (even in principle) describe to us with certainty in advance.' But this does not affect the implications of what MacKay says.

I take the implications to be as follows. Whether or not a person is morally responsible for something he does depends not on whether or not the action

[1] Vesey (1964) p. 394.

is determined, but on *how* it is determined. For it to be an action for which he is morally responsible, the determining factors (brain-processes,etc.) must be such that it is appropriate to ask him for his reasons for acting as he does. For example, if the brain-processes resulting in my foot moving as if I were kicking someone were produced by a neurologist passing an electric current through part of my brain then I would not be held to be morally responsible for the 'action'. There is a sense in which it would not be something *I* did. For a bodily movement to be one for which I can be held accountable the causal ancestry of it must not be of this 'external' kind. It must be of a kind to which there corresponds the possibility of a 'personal' accounting for the movement. Moral responsibility is opposed not to determinism as such, but only to the kind of determination I call 'external'.

In terms of this analysis, Leibniz might be represented as holding that God's creation of us, and preordination of everything we shall do, does not constitute external determination. The point could be this. Prior to being created we do not exist. And so we have no nature of our own, by contrast with which anything God might decree for us would be an external determination. The question of the determination being external or not would not arise. And so his preordination of everything we do would not be incompatible with our having freewill, in the sense of there being some things we do which are not externally determined.

If this solution of the problem of how to reconcile God's preordination with our freewill is not readily acceptable I think it must be because of our reluctance to acknowledge that we are created beings. We are reluctant to acknowledge our dependence, for being the sort of people we are, on beings other than ourselves. Johann Gottlieb Fichte (1762–1814) put it like this:

> What I desired was this: that I myself, that of which I am conscious as my own being and person, but which in this system appears as only the manifestation of a higher existence, that this 'I' would be independent, would be something which exists not by another or through another, but of myself, and, as such, would be the final root of all my determinations.[1]

What we need to do is to realize that since we are not self-created beings it is a desire which cannot be satisfied. We must be content with the sort of freedom which consists in the absence of external determination, and not hanker after the freedom of a God.

[1] Chisholm (1956) p. 27.

CHAPTER THREE

True Liberty

FREEDOM: NEGATIVE OR POSITIVE ?

In his lecture 'Two Concepts of Liberty' Sir Isaiah Berlin contrasts what he calls 'the notion of negative freedom', with 'the notion of positive freedom'.[1] Negative freedom is the freedom which Leibniz, in the dialogue in Chapter Two, is prepared to grant to Adam: 'Consider Adam just before his sin. He is free to do what he wants to do. What more can he ask?'

About positive freedom, or liberty, Berlin writes:

> The 'positive' sense of the word 'liberty' derives from the wish on the part of the individual to be his own master. I wish my life and decisions to depend on myself, not on external forces of whatever kind. I wish to be the instrument of my own, not of other men's, acts of will. I wish to be a subject, not an object; to be moved by reasons, by conscious purposes which are my own, not by causes which affect me, as it were, from outside. I wish to be somebody, not nobody; a doer – deciding, not being decided for, self-directing and not acted upon by external nature or by other men as if I were a thing, or an animal, or a slave incapable of playing a human role, that is, of conceiving goals and policies of my own and realizing them. This is at least part of what I mean when I say that I am rational, and that it is my reason that distinguishes me as a human being from the rest of the world.[2]

What makes this more than just a positive statement of the same wish for freedom as is described negatively in terms of the absence of coercion or compulsion is the emphasis on *reason*. If reason is thought of, not as David Hume (1711–1776) thought of it, as 'the slave of the passions'[3], but as a faculty that is capable of determining ends of its own, then there is the possibility of a conflict between the advocates of negative freedom (unimpeded satisfaction of natural inclinations) and of positive freedom (say, the realization of man's 'true' nature). For it may be held that man's true nature

[1] Berlin (1969) pp. 121–2.

[2] Ibid., p. 131.

[3] Selby-Bigge (1888) p. 415.

is not that of an individual, but that of a member of society. Then what is in his interests as an individual may be far removed from what is in his true interests, as a member of society. Moreover, his faculty of reason may not be sufficiently developed for him to recognize his true interests. It may seem to him that his freedom is being infringed, for the sake of some ideal he does not recognize.

In terms of Isaiah Berlin's distinction, Voltaire (1694–1778), in the dialogue that follows, is an advocate of negative freedom; Rousseau (1712–1778) is an advocate of positive freedom.

The dialogue is by Maurice Cranston, Professor of Political Science at the London School of Economics, University of London.

LIBERTY

VOLTAIRE Well, my dear Rousseau, so they are driving you out of France. Believe me, you have my sympathy. I was exceedingly sorry to hear that your *Social Contract* had been suppressed.

ROUSSEAU I should have expected you to rejoice, Voltaire. I know you disagree with everything I write.

VOLTAIRE Of course, I think you were wrong to have written the book. But they were even more wrong to have banned it.

ROUSSEAU If you think my argument is false, I don't see why you should want anyone to read it.

VOLTAIRE Because I believe in liberty.

ROUSSEAU Ah, liberty. There's one thing you and I might agree about, Voltaire, one thing in a hundred.

VOLTAIRE We might, if only you knew what liberty meant, but, alas, it is only too obvious that you don't.

ROUSSEAU By liberty I don't mean licence; as I sometimes suspect you do.

VOLTAIRE What is licence but the way other people use their liberty? The only difference between liberty and licence resides in the mind of the beholder. Both words name the same thing, but 'liberty' is used by a man who approves of what he sees, and 'licence' is used by the man who disapproves. I am not much given to disapprove, so I don't often use the word 'licence'. I leave that word to priests or to puritans, like yourself, my dear Rousseau.

ROUSSEAU I am not a puritan, except in the sense that I was born and bred in the Reformed Church of Geneva, against which I have repeatedly rebelled.

VOLTAIRE You are a true child of Calvin, all the same. The last time we met, we quarrelled, you will remember, because you wanted to have the City of Geneva forbid the opening of a theatre; and I wanted them to allow it. I was in favour of freedom, and you were against it. Our customary attitudes, Rousseau.

ROUSSEAU You say I am against freedom, Voltaire, because it is you who do not know what freedom means.

VOLTAIRE You can hardly claim to have been a champion of freedom when you demanded the suppression by the state of a cultural institution.

ROUSSEAU Theatres are not cultural institutions. They are entertainments and amusements which undermine the true culture of a people. They do not liberate; they corrupt. They are not very different from brothels. A city without theatres and brothels is freer than a city that has them. Geneva, for all its defects, has more liberty than Paris.

VOLTAIRE As one dramatist to another, I must admit it amazes me that you regard the theatre as a corrupting institution. However, you always have amazed me, Rousseau. There is a footnote in your *Social Contract* which seems to me to epitomize your extraordinary conception – or misconception – of freedom. 'In the republic of Genoa,' you write, 'the word "liberty" is inscribed on the shackles of the convicts. And this,' you add, 'is a most appropriate inscription.' There we have in brief the whole Rousseauesque philosophy of liberty: the free man is the man in chains.

ROUSSEAU Rubbish, Voltaire. I suggest that the word 'liberty' is appropriate in a prison, because the freedom of society as a whole requires the isolation of all criminals. Crime destroys freedom, just as vice does. Only a good society can be really free.

VOLTAIRE That, of course, has been said before; notably by the Catholic Inquisition. When they torture a man, they think they are bringing him back to truth and God; and they persuade themselves, in consequence, that what they are doing is setting him free.

ROUSSEAU What the Inquisition does is evil; but the argument is reasonable enough. You can force a man to be free.

VOLTAIRE Yes, I've read that phrase, too, in your *Social Contract*: a paradox, if I may say so, without wit.

ROUSSEAU It is not intended to be witty. I leave that style to writers whose trivial banalities need spice to make them acceptable.

VOLTAIRE The truth is often banal, even the truth about liberty. To be free is to be unconstrained. That is what the word 'free' means. It is all very simple and commonplace. If a man is forced he is constrained. And as he cannot logically be at the same time constrained and unconstrained, he cannot be forced to be free.

ROUSSEAU A man is free if he chooses in the full sense of choosing. If he is driven by some base passion or blinded by ignorance, he isn't really choosing. You can use force to make a man reflect upon the choice he is making, and so to exercise a rational choice. That is why it is perfectly logical to speak of forcing a man to be free.

VOLTAIRE So that is what entitles you to say that the prisoners of Genoa are free men.

ROUSSEAU I did not say that they were. I simply say that if punishment reforms a man, it helps to free him. A life of crime is a greater servitude than the shackles of a prison, because crime enslaves the soul, while visible chains only impede the movement of the body.

VOLTAIRE It is often said that a little philosophy is a dangerous thing: and it is, if it enables writers of your kind to persuade people that liberty is servitude and servitude is liberty.

ROUSSEAU That is not what I said. You don't listen.

VOLTAIRE Rousseau, I have thought about liberty for many more years than you have, I am sixty-seven and you can't yet be fifty . . .

ROUSSEAU I shall be fifty this summer, if I am allowed to live that long.

VOLTAIRE I think I began to understand what freedom really meant thirty years ago when I was an exile in England. The English know the meaning of freedom better than any other people in Europe, and there is a remark of their philosopher Thomas Hobbes which has always stuck in my mind: 'The liberty of subjects is the silence of the law.'

ROUSSEAU But Thomas Hobbes was no champion of the English notion of freedom. In fact, he wanted to turn people against it, and convert them to his own gospel of absolute sovereignty.

VOLTAIRE Perhaps he did. But that's another matter. I quoted those words because they say so well what freedom is. The more the law prohibits, the less liberty you have; and the less the law prohibits, the more liberty you have. The English are freer than the French because English law allows them to worship as they please and publish what they please and so forth. The French are less free than the English because the French laws impose the Catholic religion on the people, and censor books and all the rest of it. Hobbes sums the thing up very well when he says that 'The liberty of subjects is the silence of the law.'

ROUSSEAU You say that you learned about freedom in England, Voltaire. So wouldn't you do better to quote Locke instead of Hobbes? For isn't it Locke who is supposed to be the spokesman of the English view of liberty? If you've read Locke, you'll remember that he specifically denies what Hobbes suggests. Locke says the law doesn't diminish liberty. He says 'the law enlarges liberty.'

VOLTAIRE If you read Locke carefully, Rousseau, you will see that he used the word 'law' in a rather special and limited sense. By 'law' he does not mean the system of imposed law that is upheld in this or that kingdom or republic. By 'law' Locke means only those rules that rational men will agree to live by. He denies the dignity of the name of law to the edicts of unjust rulers. But Hobbes uses the word 'law' in a much more familiar way, as he himself explains, meaning the command of the sovereign. By 'sovereign' of course he means the ruler and all the agencies of government. Any imposed law is law in Hobbes's sense. So if we are content to use Hobbes's words in the way he uses them, we must surely agree with him that the more the law commands or forbids, the less free the people are.

ROUSSEAU I do not agree with you, Voltaire, any more than I agree with Hobbes. But I am quite pleased to hear you quote his authority, because I have often thought you were rather like him in your zeal for enlightened despotism.

VOLTAIRE I have no *zeal* for enlightened despotism. I accept it as a political necessity for France due to its particular historical condition which you as a Swiss don't understand. Sovereignty in France isn't single and undivided as it is in some other constitutions. The King is not the only centre of power here, by any means. There are other sources of constraint, such as the Church and the feudal nobility, which bear much more heavily upon the people than any King of France has ever done. So clearly the enlargement of men's liberties in France requires the suppression of these other oppressive institutions. And only a King could undertake that task.

ROUSSEAU I cannot see why you object to my words about forcing men to be free, when you claim that that is exactly what your enlightened despotism is intended to do: to use force to bring about a situation in which men are free.

VOLTAIRE But that isn't forcing anyone to be free. It's a matter of using force to destroy the enemies of freedom, which is a very different and more profitable enterprise. Like Locke, I see that freedom in this world can never be absolute. We cannot ask for total liberty, but only for as much liberty as possible.

ROUSSEAU I wouldn't deny that the laws are less oppressive in England, and that Englishmen think they are free. And perhaps at election times, when they are choosing their rulers, they are free, but most of the time they are not free, because they live under laws that are made by their King and Parliament. Free men are men who make their own laws.

VOLTAIRE Parliament represents the people.

ROUSSEAU It claims to, but it doesn't, because once they have been elected the Members of Parliament turn themselves from servants into masters. No man can represent another in legislating. If men are to be free, they must all legislate, directly and in person.

VOLTAIRE But how can that be done, except in some ancient Greek democracy?

ROUSSEAU It is still done in some Swiss cantons: and it could be done in other places, if people knew what freedom meant. And it doesn't mean being left alone by the law: it means taking an active part in making law.

VOLTAIRE But, my dear Rousseau, even in the curious narrative which you relate in your *Social Contract*, the people is sovereign in only a very nominal sense. You have the people enact the laws, admittedly: but they are laws which have been drawn up for them by an outsider called the lawmaker, and then the laws are administered by magistrates.

ROUSSEAU At the beginning of the book I explain what I am trying to do: to outline the institutions which would enable men as they are to be both free and ruled. And ordinary men as they are now are too ignorant to draw up codes of law.

VOLTAIRE Of course they are: and isn't your law-giver as much an enlightened despot as any king that I might favour?

ROUSSEAU I visualize the law-giver persuading people, not commanding them.

VOLTAIRE In a word he must have their consent: which is exactly what a constitutional monarch has. You tell me I recommend, without knowing it, forcing men to be free: I tell you, that you recommend, without admitting it, an enlightened despotism more despotic than anything I would tolerate.

ROUSSEAU There is a vast difference between us. You would have people invest sovereignty in a monarch; I insist that they must keep it themselves.

VOLTAIRE I realize, Rousseau, that like all Genevans you set great store by words like 'republic' and 'the sovereignty of the people'. But what all this splendid language signifies is that in Geneva there is no single royal dynasty, but a council of rich bourgeois families at the head of the state. Instead of a monarchy you have an oligarchy, and unfortunately it is not an especially enlightened one.

ROUSSEAU You can speak as scornfully as you please of Geneva, but I notice you have made your home on the very borders of it, so that you can escape into that city if the French authorities turn against you.

VOLTAIRE And back over the border again if the need should arise. But it is hardly for you to reproach me for that, my dear Rousseau, since I well know that you are on your way to Neuchâtel to seek the protection of my former friend, King Frederick of Prussia, an enlightened despot in his own eyes, if no longer so enlightened in mine.

ROUSSEAU I am hunted, Voltaire, like a deer. I cannot always pause to ask who owns the land where I shelter.

VOLTAIRE You should let yourself be hunted like a fox, as I have been, and then you might learn some of its cunning.

ROUSSEAU I have no wish to be cunning. I hate falsehood, dissembling, insincerity of any kind. In fact I don't believe that anyone can understand what freedom means if he doesn't love goodness. Only the good man can be truly free.

VOLTAIRE It is enough to be free; there is no need to be 'truly' free. A good man is a man who makes better use of his freedom, but a bad man has just as much freedom, if his external circumstances are the same. Freedom is not the exclusive privilege of the virtuous: and let us hope that it will never be, for otherwise there would be very few free men in the world.

ROUSSEAU But how can you in seriousness dismiss the connection between liberty and goodness?

VOLTAIRE I don't dismiss it but it too quickly becomes a metaphysical question that you and I could dispute for ever and never settle. Now the question 'Is an Englishman more free than a Frenchman?' is a political question, and one to which I think one can give a very definite answer. Even you who don't think that the English are free to the extent that they could be, even you, Rousseau, would agree with me that they are at least more free than we French are.

ROUSSEAU Their rulers are undoubtedly more tolerant.

VOLTAIRE And you would agree that that is something to be valued?

ROUSSEAU Yes, in a certain sense, it is. I may even find myself obliged to throw myself upon their liberality, and seek refuge in England, as you once did.

VOLTAIRE And if you do, I hope you will learn as much as I once learned in England about liberty as a principle of practical politics. When you say, my dear Rousseau, that freedom is possible only in a community of good men ruling themselves, you are talking as a philosopher, about things which exist in the mind. When I say, we must have liberty in France, I really only mean that we ought to have in France what the English have in England, or something like it.

ROUSSEAU But why ask for such an impoverished simulacrum of liberty. Why not ask for liberty itself?

VOLTAIRE You may call it an impoverished simulacrum of liberty, but that is not how it appears to me. Not when I see my books suppressed here in France, and freely sold in England; not when I see my Protestant friends in France subjected to judicial murder, or tortured, or imprisoned – as I have in far too many cases; and then look at England and see every kind of heterodox religion flourish unmolested. No, my dear Rousseau, freedom loses none of its enchantment for me for being, as it must necessarily be, a partial liberty.

ROUSSEAU Partial liberty is not a genuine liberty. Men are either free or they are not free. If they content themselves with what you call partial liberty, they will never know what real freedom is.

VOLTAIRE But there I think you are greatly mistaken. It is not at all a case in politics of men being free or not free: they can either be less free or more free: they will never be absolutely free: the reasonable thing to aim for is to get as much liberty as can be got. To abandon the impossible, and to have as much as one can of the possible.

ROUSSEAU You make an eloquent plea for compromise, Voltaire. As you have always done. A rebel of the drawing room. But somehow I don't think France will be content for long with what you offer. I think when the French get fired with the desire for liberty, they will want the whole thing: a republic like that of ancient Rome, where every man is a citizen and the citizen makes the laws.

VOLTAIRE And if they want it, will they achieve it?

ROUSSEAU It is easy to institute liberty: the problem is to keep it.

VOLTAIRE Do you think the difficulties will be overcome?

ROUSSEAU No, Voltaire, I am not an optimist.

VOLTAIRE Ah, but I am. I ask for less than you. But I not only hope, I expect to see it realized.

ROUSSEAU At the age of sixty-seven?

VOLTAIRE I intend to be immortal.

ROUSSEAU Then you have some faith, after all, in the life after death?

VOLTAIRE An ounce of faith.

ROUSSEAU A mere ounce of faith and a plenitude of hope. Voltaire, no wonder they call you the voice of this age. I am unlike the rest of you. I have an infinite measure of faith, but hardly any hope at all.

VOLTAIRE Well, that I am afraid is your misfortune. You should pray, as I do, to have your faith removed, and your hope restored.

GUIDE TO FURTHER READING

A convenient edition of Rousseau's *Social Contract* is the translation by Maurice Cranston. Some of Cranston's own ideas on liberty are developed in his book, *Freedom*.

Mention has already been made of Sir Isaiah Berlin's *Four Essays on Liberty*. Two other books worth reading in connection with the dialogue are Peter Gay's *Voltaire's Politics* and Judith N. Shklar's *Men and Citizens: a Study of Rousseau's Social Theory*.

In the dialogue Rousseau says 'A man is free if he chooses in the full sense of choosing.' Choosing 'in the full sense' means exercising a rational choice. Someone who is 'driven by some base passion' is not really choosing.

The philosopher who has developed this distinction – between reason, on the one hand, and passion, or inclination, on the other – most systematically is Immanuel Kant (1724–1804). Kant was deeply influenced by Rousseau. Indeed, Book 1, Chapter 8 of Rousseau's *Social Contract* can be read as an introduction to Kant's moral philosophy. With Kant one is getting into fairly deep waters, philosophically. If you buy Immanuel Kant's *The Moral Law*, then you should also buy a commentary, such as Oswald Hanfling's *Kant's Copernican Revolution: Moral Philosophy*.

CHAPTER FOUR

The Reasonable Moralist

ARE MORAL TERMS DESCRIPTIVE OF THE WORLD ?

At the end of Chapter Three I mentioned Kant's *The Moral Law*. One formulation of his moral law was 'Act only on that maxim through which you can at the same time will that it should become a universal law.' Grammatically this is in the imperative mood. It expresses a command or exhortation, as opposed to pointing out, stating, or declaring something. Moreover it is a categorical imperative. It is not of the form '*If* you want such and such, *then* act thus'. It is of the form 'Act thus'.

A present-day moral philosopher whose views have something in common with those of Kant is R. M. Hare, White's Professor of Moral Philosophy in the University of Oxford. Hare holds that a moral utterance can be characterized in terms of *prescriptivity* and *universalizability*.[1] The universalizability requirement is very Kantian, but 'prescriptive' is opposed not, like 'imperative', to 'indicative', but to 'descriptive'.

Calling moral language prescriptive, as opposed to descriptive, can be regarded as one way out of a quandary that found expression in the moral philosophy of G. E. Moore (1873–1958). Moore drew attention to the difference between saying, for example, that actions which produce the greatest happiness of the greatest number are right and saying that the word 'right' as applied to actions simply *means* productive of the greatest happiness of the greatest number. If the latter were true, Moore says, then right would be a *natural* characteristic. Statements including moral terms, like 'right' and 'good', would be analysable in terms of 'natural' things, like happiness; and in saying 'Happiness is good' we would be saying something as uninformative as 'Brothers are male'. It seemed to Moore to be evident that utterances like 'Actions which produce the greatest happiness of the greatest number are right' are *not*, if true, analytic. And he accordingly said that moral terms refer

[1] This is a slight over-simplification. See the footnote on p. 47.

to *non*-natural characteristics. They are descriptive, but they do not describe things in natural terms.

Having said this he had to explain what he meant by 'non-natural'. He said that a 'natural object' is any object that is capable of existing in time, and that a 'natural characteristic' of a natural object could be conceived as existing in time all by itself. A 'non-natural characteristic', then, was one of which this was not true.

A colleague, C. D. Broad (1887–1971) remarked that *every* characteristic of a natural object answers to Moore's criterion of non-naturalness, and that *no* characteristic could possibly be natural in his sense.

He wrote:

> I do not believe for a moment that . . . the brownness or roundness of a penny could exist in time all by itself. Hence, if I accepted Moore's account, I should have to reckon brownness, roundness, pleasantness, etc., as *non-natural* characteristics. Yet he certainly counts them as *natural* characteristics.[1]

Moore, with good grace, conceded that he had not given any tenable explanation of what he meant by saying that 'good' was a non-natural characteristic.

Broad suggested a way out of the difficulty:

> A complete discussion of this doctrine [the doctrine that 'good' is a name of a non-natural characteristic] would have to begin by raising a question which Moore never did raise but which has become acute in recent years. Is 'good' a name of a characteristic at all? Or do sentences like 'This is good', though grammatically similar to sentences like 'This is yellow' which undoubtedly ascribe a certain characteristic to a subject, really need an entirely different kind of analysis? Is it not possible that the function of such sentences is to express or to stimulate certain kinds of emotion, or to command or forbid certain kinds of action, and not to state certain kinds of fact?[2]

In this passage Broad mentions two alternatives to holding that moral terms like 'good' are descriptive. The first is that sentences like 'This is good' function 'to express or to stimulate certain kinds of emotion.' 'Good' does not describe whatever 'this' is; it functions to express the emotion of the speaker or to evoke a like emotion in the person addressed. 'This is good' is not descriptive; it is expressive or evocative. The name 'emotivism' has been given to this doctrine of the function of moral utterances.

The second alternative to Moore's 'descriptivism' is 'prescriptivism', the

[1] Broad (1942) p. 59.

[2] Broad (1942) p. 58.

doctrine that 'This is good' functions to prescribe or prohibit certain kinds of action.

R. M. Hare is not an emotivist; he is a prescriptivist. One of his reasons for rejecting emotivism is, I think, that when the emotivist has to say what *kinds* of emotion are expressed or evoked, he cannot do so without falling back on moral concepts. He may say that the emotion is one of approval, but, Hare remarks,

> 'I approve of A' is merely a more complicated and circumlocutory way of saying 'A is right'. It is not a statement, verifiable by observation, that I have a recognizable feeling or recurrent frame of mind; it is a value-judgement; if I ask 'Do I approve of A?' my answer is a moral decision, not an observation of introspective fact.[1]

A second reason Hare may have for rejecting emotivism is that the emphasis in it on emotion draws attention away from the other feature which he holds to characterize moral utterances. This is the feature of 'universalizability'. This feature is important because, he holds, it is the feature which distinguishes moral utterances from imperatives in the ordinary sense, and which makes reasoning in morals possible.

In the discussion that follows Hare explains and defends his view that the meaning of 'ought' statements is determined by their being 'prescriptive' and 'universalizable'. He is questioned by Anthony Kenny, Fellow of Balliol College, Oxford.

WHAT USE IS MORAL PHILOSOPHY?

KENNY Professor Hare, before we start our discussion, I wonder if you could give the students a statement of your basic position. You mentioned in a preface of a recent book that you were first interested in moral philosophy because of an interest in actual moral problems. What was it that started you off?

HARE Well, I suppose it happened just before and during the Second World War. In the 'thirties there was a lot of unemployment, a lot of poverty, much worse than anything that's happening here now. And it raised problems about inequalities of wealth, for example; and then there was the problem of war itself: whether it is ever right to fight. And, of course,

---

[1] Hare (1952) pp. 6–7.

behind these there loomed bigger problems about what one's purpose ought to be in life anyway. These were moral problems, all boiling down to questions of what one ought to do; and they were pressing because one had to *decide* what to do, for example, whether to join the army when Hitler started his war. I never thought of moral problems as anything else but extremely practical ones. Perhaps that's why I became a prescriptivist.

I only became clear about how philosophy could help after the war, though I was thinking a lot about philosophy during it. It became clear to me that the first step in tackling any difficult question is to understand what it is you're asking; and this involves knowing the meaning of the words in the question. I came to this conclusion partly, I suppose, as a result of reading what Plato said about Socrates, who started the business, and partly as a result of contact with the new school of analytical philosophy. I thought that if one was to answer questions about what one ought to do, one had to know what 'ought' meant, and I realized that I didn't begin to know what it meant. And to try to find out what it meant was doing moral philosophy.

Another reason why we have to find out what such words mean is that only then shall we be clear about their logical properties; and we won't be able to tell whether arguments about what we ought to do are good arguments or bad arguments until we know what the logical properties of the words are, for only in that way can we tell what follows from what, what propositions are consistent with one another, and so on. So philosophical analysis really is indispensable if we're going to get to the bottom of any difficult problem in morality; though I don't say that it is the only thing we have to do, because usually there are very difficult factual questions involved too, about the consequences of the alternative actions. I'll try and show you what I mean, by taking the word 'ought', because it's perhaps the simplest of these words. What I think I've discovered – I don't think I was the first person to discover it – is that this word has two properties which together determine its meaning. First of all, I don't say it's 'emotive' – that would be quite wrong – but prescriptive. This means that for any 'ought'-statement there's something that counts as acting in accordance with it, and that if you don't so act, when the occasion arises, you can't really and sincerely subscribe to it (unless of course you're unable to act as it requires). The second logical property that 'ought'-statements have is what has been called their universalizability (I apologize for these long words). By this I mean that if I say that someone ought to do something, it has to be because of something about him and his situation, and that if this something were to be true of any other person and any other situation, I couldn't without inconsistency deny that the person in that other situation ought to do the same. In fact, moral judgements rest on principles (perhaps complex principles) applying to all situations of a certain kind. And it's these principles that we are really subscribing to when we make moral judgements.

Now, in my first book, *The Language of Morals*, I was trying to establish that moral judgements have these two properties. And in my second book, *Freedom and Reason*, I was trying to show how a theory of moral reasoning can be founded on these properties.

KENNY Both these books have been extremely influential: in this country and abroad people have looked at many questions in moral philosophy quite differently as a result of reading them. But I'd like to focus, if I may, on some of the criticisms that have been made of your position. I don't think that people really want to contest – not in this country at any rate – that moral judgements are universalizable. I for my own part wouldn't want to contest that they are prescriptive if all that means is that they have consequences for action. But I am rather doubtful whether these two characteristics of being prescriptive and universalizable are sufficient to characterize what is special about morality and moral judgements.

Can I just go over the distinction which you make between 'is'-statements and 'ought'-statements to see that I've got it right? You have, first of all, 'is'-statements which are descriptive; they describe things, they say what the world is like, and they're universalizable. If I describe this piece of paper as white, I have to describe as white anything which it resembles in the relevant respects. At the other extreme, you have imperatives, commands: these are prescriptive (that is they tell us what to do) but they're non-universalizable. If I ask you to pass the butter, this is prescriptive (it tells you something to do) but it isn't universalizable (I don't mean that everybody situated as you are has to pass the butter). In between these we have 'ought'-statements: they share with imperatives the characteristic of being prescriptive and with 'is'-statements the property of being universalizable. Is that fair as a statement of your position?

HARE Well, I think I'd accept it as a summary statement. Of course one has to over-simplify.[1]

KENNY Naturally. Now the question I want to put to you is whether this is really an adequate characterization of moral judgements. Suppose that a

---

[1] In particular, there are some (off-colour) 'oughts' which are moral but not prescriptive (see R. M. Hare, *Freedom and Reason*, pp. 26f., 52f.), and some value-judgements which are not moral but still prescriptive and universalizable (*op. cit.*, pp. 139f.). For 'over-ridingness' as a mark distinguishing moral from other evaluative judgements, see below and *op. cit.*, pp. 168f.

society had a set of dietary precepts: one was not to eat beans, say, or one was not to eat cabbage. Naturally these would be regarded as prescriptive judgements; obviously there would be conclusions to be drawn about action: not to eat beans, not to eat cabbage. And suppose they were universalizable; suppose these people believed very firmly that human beings, all human beings, should refrain from eating beans or eating cabbage. Now it seems to me that if this was all we were told about the people in this society, we couldn't yet say that this was a moral system that they had.

HARE Well, I think I should like to say to that that I don't attach enormous importance to the word 'moral'. What I attach importance to is having a set of principles to live by. Now, I don't care frightfully whether you call them moral or not; but if these people you describe who won't eat beans, really stuck to not eating beans through thick and thin (in the same way as that in which some people even nowadays stick to certain sexual taboos), and let that principle override all sorts of principles *we* call moral principles, then I think we should call them moral principles, just as people call these sexual principles moral principles.

KENNY You say if these people allowed the non-eating of beans to override things which we would call moral principles, then we might say that they had a moral system too. I think I agree with that, but it seems to me that now the crucial point is: what are the reasons why we call the overridden principles *moral* principles. And I put it to you that there must be something else besides being prescriptive and universalizable which makes us call the things we call moral principles by that name.

HARE Excuse me, I don't think that's really the question at all. I think the question is not why we call them moral principles, but why we accept those moral principles and don't accept the moral principles like not eating beans. They're both moral principles; and I think an explanation should be given of why we or why I don't include the thing about not eating beans in my set of moral principles. Well, if anybody did, I would say that he held a very extraordinary moral principle, but still a moral principle.

KENNY It would be enough to make it a moral principle merely that he held it in this way?

HARE It would be enough to make it *his* moral principle. I would say of him that he was holding it as a moral principle if he really stuck to it like that, like people stick to the rules against incest for example. I can imagine a culture which regarded the rule against incest in much the light in which ours regards the rule against eating beans. And two people in that culture might be having the same discussion we're now having, with the examples turned round; and you would be saying to me 'Suppose somebody thought it frightfully wrong to, say, go to bed with his sister; could you really call that a moral principle?'

KENNY You don't think that there has to be anything about the *content* of a judgement in order to make it a moral judgement? It doesn't have to have any connection with human welfare or happiness or anything like that?

HARE Not in order to make it a moral judgement. Once one has accepted the formal properties which I say moral judgement has (namely prescriptivity and universalizability), I think I can give you very good reasons why we all accept the moral principles that we do, which nearly all of them have something to do with human happiness. But I refrain from writing this into the definition of the word 'moral' simply because I do wish to be able to argue with people, and one does meet people who don't think of human happiness as of prime importance. Nietzschians, for example. I want to be able to have an argument with them; I want to start far enough back, as it were, in order to catch them into the argument so that I can use the purely formal properties of the words in order to reason with them. If we rule them out at the beginning as not having moral opinions at all, the argument can never begin; they would go on with their opinions, we would have ours, and we couldn't reason with them.

KENNY If you restrict yourself to the purely formal properties in that way, then it isn't at all clear what reason anybody has for adopting morality at all, for talking the type of language, I mean, which is characterized by the formal properties you mentioned. If morality is closely connected with human happiness then one can see why somebody either for prudential reasons or benevolent reasons would have an interest in talking about morality. But if morality need not as such have any connection with happiness, why should anyone trouble about moral language?

HARE Well, the beauty of it is that when the moral words are defined in terms of their formal properties, although we haven't written anything about human happiness into their definition, nevertheless we can see extremely good reasons why people should want to have a set of words in their language having those properties. If you are trying with the other people in your society to come to a set of principles which you can all accept, that is to say, if you're trying to find kinds of behaviour that all of you can prescribe universally for the behaviour of all of you, then you don't start with any content which is going to be written into your definition of morality, but you just start off with those formal properties. It's obvious, I think, why people will be likely to accept a set of such universal principles for their behaviour as will be directed towards an increase in human happiness. Isn't this obvious?

KENNY I think that it's obvious that they will be keen to increase human happiness, but whether they will think that this is best done by adopting a particular style of the use of language is, I think, rather a different matter.

Perhaps I could connect this with something that seems to me to have been a development in your own interests over the years. In *The Language of Morals* you were interested mainly, I think, in an ethical problem, the problem of the nature of moral judgement, the philosophical problem about the distinction between moral judgements and other sorts of judgements. You described yourself as a prescriptivist and you named your opponents 'descriptivists' – descriptivists being people who thought that moral judgements were in some way judgements about the world, judgements that told us how the world was. You, as a prescriptivist, said: No, when one is making a moral judgement, one is essentially prescribing for oneself and for others. Now that's an ethical distinction, a distinction about the nature of moral language.

There is another, moral, distinction which can be contrasted with this: that is the distinction between absolutist moralities and consequentialist moralities. Let me explain what I mean. An absolutist is somebody who thinks that there are certain types of action which should never be done no matter what the consequences. He may say, for instance, nobody should ever be judicially tortured, no matter what would be the consequences of not torturing him. A consequentialist, by contrast, might say we can't decide in advance whether torture is right or wrong; in any particular case we must try to assess the consequences of torturing somebody or not torturing him. The classical utilitarians, I think, Bentham and Mill, were consequentialists in this way.

Now you can combine these two distinctions in various ways. You can be a prescriptivist absolutist or you can be a prescriptivist consequentialist, and you can combine consequentialism with prescriptivism or with descriptivism.

You yourself, if I understand rightly, are a prescriptivist consequentialist.

HARE Well, I'll be able to determine that when I understand your distinction better. I'm inclined to think that, at any rate in most senses of absolutist, I'm an absolutist. For example, I'm not a relativist, but that, I think, is not the distinction you're making. I don't really see why a person who assigns importance to the consequences of actions – what you're *doing* when you're

doing something – can't be called an absolutist in any sense I would understand. I mean a person, for example, who thinks that one absolutely ought
not to bring about pain in somebody else by torture – isn't that a consequence that one's forbidden to bring about?

KENNY Certainly one can be absolutist about some things and not others. The
same person might be an absolutist about torture and say that torture is
absolutely wrong (meaning by this that once any action falls under the
description 'torture' you don't need to know anything more about it to
know that it's wrong) and yet not be, say, an absolutist about lying; he
might think that some lies were all right, some lies were not, and one ought
to know more about a particular case in order to judge.

I'd like to ask you, not now as a moral philosopher, but as a moralist,
whether you are in fact an absolutist about torture. Do you think torture is
always and absolutely wrong?

HARE Well, it's hard to answer that question until you tell me what I'm
allowed to include under 'always'. I can think up situations, entirely
fantastic ones if you like, in which I would think it right to torture somebody in order to extract information from him. I give an example of this
in one of my books.[1] But I don't think that such situations are likely to
occur. Even if they do occur I think that, once the people who are in
charge of these things (say, members of the police force) get it into their
heads that it is sometimes legitimate to torture a prisoner, they will so
easily persuade themselves that the particular case which confronts them is
one of these cases, that it is very much the best thing if they simply rule it
out from their minds. The point here is: I'm not against these rather
simple principles which I think are what the absolutist is really after. I'm
not against them; the quarrel is one about their status.

KENNY Doesn't this mean that you think that the philosophers should really
deceive the policemen? You as a philosopher, having studied the hypothetical cases, can see that torture isn't always wrong, but you think it
would be a good thing if the policeman believed it was always wrong. Is
that right?

HARE Well, here you're importing the question of belief, aren't you? I don't
like to talk in those terms, but I think it would be a good thing if the
policeman (or I, if I were a policeman, even if I did philosophy sometimes
when I wasn't being a policeman) put the idea of torture out of his head;
and this is a perfectly consistent position for a philosopher to hold. As a

[1] Hare (1963) p. 43. See also Hare (1973) and (1972c).

philosopher I can say: Well, there might be fantastic situations in which it would be right to torture people; but once I get into my constable's uniform, or whatever policemen wear, I must just put it out of my head, because although it's conceivable that such cases might occur, they're very unlikely to occur. And if I once let myself think they might occur and that this case might be one of them, then I shall find myself doing it.

KENNY I'm interested that you didn't like talking about believing that torture was always wrong. I take it that on your view when you express what I would call a moral belief, what I can get from this is not any information about the world, but only information about you. If you tell me that torture is always wrong, all I can really learn from this is a certain resolution that you have taken rather than anything about the world.

HARE Well, in the same sense that if I tell you that the train left five minutes ago, all you can get, from listening to me say that, is information about what I believe about the train.

KENNY No, because if I think that your belief has been correctly arrived at – and knowing you to be the kind of person you are, I would assume it had been – I can get the further information that the train leaves at that time.

HARE Well then, let's be quite clear about this. There are at least two things that happen when I tell you the thing about the train. One is: you, from my behaviour, gather that I believe something, and that's a piece of information. You also, if I'm an honest man and well informed, gather some information about the train. Now, if I tell you that I think that torturing is always wrong, you get, parallel to the first of those, some information about what I think about torturing. The second thing that happens, however is different. What I have conveyed to you and what, if you agree with me, you will think, will be that *torturing is wrong*, which is something prescriptive.

KENNY But I don't get any information about any objective moral values, and I think that this is what some of your critics have had in mind when they say that your view annihilates moral values. You denied that it does this, but it seems to me that you do annihilate moral values in the same sense as somebody annihilates Santa Claus when he tells a child that Santa Claus doesn't exist.

HARE Of course, it would be an awful pity to annihilate Santa Claus if Santa Claus was doing any good, but if either he didn't exist or he wasn't doing any good, or if the belief in him might have been of positive harm, then it wouldn't be a bad thing that people should learn that he doesn't exist and learn to get on without him.[1]

KENNY Thank you very much, Professor Hare.

GUIDE TO FURTHER READING

The two books by R. M. Hare referred to in the discussion are *The Language of Morals* and *Freedom and Reason*.

One of the main issues raised in the discussion is whether the two characteristics 'of being prescriptive and being universalizable are sufficient to characterize what is special about morality and moral judgements'. Kenny asks whether there has not also to be something about the *content* of a judgement, such as a connection with human welfare or happiness, in order to make it a moral judgement. A philosopher who would argue in favour of such a content is Philippa Foot. Her paper on 'Moral Beliefs' together with an Appendix to it from her introduction to *Theories of Ethics*, is reprinted in *Fundamental Problems in Philosophy*, edited by Oswald Hanfling. Reprinted in the same volume is a critical discussion of the position Miss Foot holds, by D. Z. Phillips and H. O. Mounce, entitled 'On Morality's having a Point'.

A related issue raised in the discussion is that of the connection between moral words being defined in terms of their formal properties and people's behaviour being directed towards an increase in human happiness. Hare says the connection is obvious. Kenny evidently has doubts about it. Hare has set out the argument for a connection in a paper 'Wrongness and Harm' in *Essays on the Moral Concepts*, pages 92–109. The core of the argument is on pages 100–3.

[1] See '"Nothing Matters": Is "the Annihilation of Values" something that could happen?', in Hare (1972a).

CHAPTER FIVE

Brain Transplants and Personal Identity

BRAIN TRANSPLANTS

In 1973 in the *Sunday Times* there was a report of how a team from the Metropolitan Hospital in Cleveland under Dr R. J. White had successfully transplanted a monkey's head on to another monkey's body.[1] Dr White was reported as having said, 'Technically a human head transplant is possible', and as hoping that 'it may be possible eventually to transplant *parts* of the brain or other organs inside the head'.

The possibility of brain transplants gives rise to a fascinating philosophical problem. Imagine the following situation:

> Two men, a Mr Brown and a Mr Robinson, had been operated on for brain tumours and brain extractions had been performed on both of them. At the end of the operations, however, the assistant inadvertently put Brown's brain in Robinson's head, and Robinson's brain in Brown's head. One of these men immediately dies, but the other, the one with Robinson's body and Brown's brain, eventually regains consciousness. Let us call the latter 'Brownson'. Upon regaining consciousness Brownson exhibits great shock and surprise at the appearance of his body. Then, upon seeing Brown's body, he exclaims incredulously 'That's me lying there!' Pointing to himself he says 'This isn't my body; the one over there is!' When asked his name he automatically replies 'Brown'. He recognizes Brown's wife and family (whom Robinson had never met), and is able to describe in detail events in Brown's life, always describing them as events in his own life. Of Robinson's past life he evinces no knowledge at all. Over a period of time he is observed to display all of the personality traits, mannerisms, interests, likes and dislikes, and so on, that had previously characterized Brown, and to act and talk in ways completely alien to the old Robinson.[2]

The next step is to suppose that Brown's brain is not simply transplanted whole into someone else's brainless head, but is divided in two and half put

---

[1] *Sunday Times*, 9 December, 1973, p. 13.

[2] Shoemaker (1963) pp. 23–4.

into each of *two* other people's brainless heads. The same memory having been coded in many parts of the cortex, they *both* then say they are Brown, are able to describe events in Brown's life as if they are events in their own lives, etc. What should we say now?

The implications of this case for what we should say about personal identity are considered by Derek Parfit in a paper entitled 'Personal Identity'. Parfit's own view is expressed in terms of a relationship he calls 'psychological continuity'. He analyses this relationship partly in terms of what he calls '*q*-memory' ('*q*' stands for 'quasi'). He sketches a definition of '*q*-memory' as follows:

> I am *q*-remembering an experience if (1) I have a belief about a past experience which seems in itself like a memory belief, (2) someone did have such an experience, and (3) my belief is dependent upon this experience in the same way (whatever that is) in which a memory of an experience is dependent upon it.[1]

The significance of this definition of *q*-memory is that *two* people can, in theory, *q*-remember doing what only one person did. So two people can, in theory, be psychologically continuous with one person.

Parfit's thesis is that there is nothing more to personal identity than this 'psychological continuity'. This is *not* to say that whenever there is a sufficient degree of psychological continuity there is personal identity, for psychological continuity could be a one-two, or 'branching', relationship, and we are able to speak of 'identity' only when there is a one-one relationship. It *is* to say that a common belief – in the special nature of personal identity – is mistaken.

In the discussion that follows I began by asking Parfit what he thinks of this common belief. Derek Parfit is a Fellow of All Souls, Oxford.

PERSONAL IDENTITY

VESEY Derek, can we begin with the belief that you claim most of us have about personal identity? It's this: whatever happens between now and some future time either I shall still exist or I shan't. And any future experience will either be my experience or it won't. In other words, personal identity is an all or nothing matter: either I survive or I don't. Now what do you want to say about that?

PARFIT It seems to me just false. I think the true view is that we can easily describe and imagine large numbers of cases in which the question, 'Will

---

[1] Parfit (1971) p. 15.

that future person be me – or someone else?', is both a question which doesn't have any answer at all, and there's no puzzle that there's no answer.

VESEY Will you describe one such case.

PARFIT One of them is the case discussed in the correspondence material, the case of division in which we suppose that each half of my brain is to be transplanted into a new body and the two resulting people will both seem to remember the whole of my life, have my character and be psychologically continuous with me in every way. Now in this case of division there were only three possible answers to the question, 'What's going to happen to *me*?' And all three of them seem to me open to very serious objections.' So the conclusion to be drawn from the case is that the question of what's going to happen to me, just doesn't have an answer. I think the case also shows that that's not mysterious at all.

VESEY Right, let's deal with these three possibilities in turn.

PARFIT Well, the first is that I'm going to be both of the resulting people. What's wrong with that answer is that it leads very quickly to a contradiction.

VESEY How?

PARFIT The two resulting people are going to be different people from each other. They're going to live completely different lives. They're going to be as different as any two people are. But if they're different people from each other it can't be the case that I'm going to be both of them. Because if I'm both of them, then one of the resulting people is going to be the same person as the other.

VESEY Yes. They can't be different people and be the same person, namely me.

PARFIT Exactly. So the first answer leads to a contradiction.

VESEY Yes. And the second?

PARFIT Well, the second possible answer is that I'm not going to be both of them but just one of them. This doesn't lead to a contradiction, it's just wildly implausible. It's implausible because my relation to each of the resulting people is exactly similar.

VESEY Yes, so there's no reason to say that I'm one rather than the other?

PARFIT It just seems absurd to suppose that, when you've got exactly the same relation, one of them is identity and the other is nothing at all.

VESEY It does seem absurd, but there are philosophers who would say that sort of thing. Let's go on to the third.

PARFIT Well, the only remaining answer, if I'm not going to be both of them or only one of them, is that I'm going to be neither of them. What's wrong with this answer is that it's grossly misleading.

VESEY Why?

PARFIT If I'm going to be neither of them, then there's not going to be anyone in the world after the operation who's going to be me. And that implies, given the way we now think, that the operation is as bad as death. Because if there's going to be no one who's going to be me, then I cease to exist. But it's obvious on reflection that the operation isn't as bad as death. It isn't bad in any way at all. That this is obvious can be shown by supposing that when they do the operation only one of the transplants succeeds and only one of the resulting people ever comes to consciousness again.

VESEY Then I think we would say that this person is me. I mean we'd have no reason to say that he wasn't.

PARFIT On reflection I'm sure we would all think that I would survive as that one person.

VESEY Yes.

PARFIT Yes. Well, if we now go back to the case where both operations succeed . . .

VESEY Where there's a double success . . .

PARFIT It's clearly absurd to suppose that a double success is a failure.

VESEY Yes.

PARFIT So the conclusion that I would draw from this case is firstly, that to the question, 'What's going to happen to me?', there's no true answer.

VESEY Yes.

PARFIT Secondly, that if we decide to say one of the three possible answers, what we say is going to obscure the true nature of the case.

VESEY Yes.

PARFIT And, thirdly, the case isn't in any way puzzling. And the reason for that is this. My relation to each of the resulting people is the relation of full psychological continuity. When I'm psychologically continuous with only one person, we call it identity. But if I'm psychologically continuous with two future people, we can't call it identity. It's not puzzling because we know exactly what's going to happen.

VESEY Yes, could I see if I've got this straight? Where there is psychological continuity in a one-one case, this is the sort of case which we'd ordinarily talk of in terms of a person having survived the operation, or something like that.

PARFIT Yes.

VESEY Now what about when there is what you call psychological continuity – that's to say, where the people seem to remember having been me and so on – in a one-two case? Is this survival or not?

PARFIT Well, I think it's just as good as survival, but the block we have to get over is that we can't say that anyone in the world after the operation is going to be me.

VESEY No.

PARFIT Well, we can say it but it's very implausible. And we're inclined to think that if there's not going to be anyone who is me tomorrow, then I don't survive. What we need to realize is that my relation to each of those two people is just as good as survival. Nothing is missing at all in my relation to both of them, as compared with my relation to myself to-morrow.

VESEY Yes.

PARFIT So here we've got survival without identity. And that only seems puzzling if we think that identity is a further fact over and above psychological continuity.

VESEY It is very hard not to think of identity being a further fact, isn't it?

PARFIT Yes, I think it is. I think that the only way to get rid of our temptation to believe this is to consider many more cases than this one case of division. Perhaps I should give you another one. Suppose that the following is going to happen to me. When I die in a normal way, scientists are going to map the states of all the cells in my brain and body and after a few months they will have constructed a perfect duplicate of me out of organic matter. And this duplicate will wake up fully psychologically continuous with me, seeming to remember my life with my character, etc.

VESEY Yes.

PARFIT Now in this case, which is a secular version of the Resurrection, we're very inclined to think that the following question arises and is very real and very important. The question is, 'Will that person who wakes up in three months be me or will he be some quite other person who's merely artificially made to be exactly like me?'

VESEY It does seem to be a real question. I mean in the one case, if it is going to be me, then I have expectations and so on, and in the other case, where it isn't me, I don't.

PARFIT I agree, it seems as if there couldn't be a bigger difference between it being me and it being someone else.

VESEY But you want to say that the two possibilities are in fact the same?

PARFIT I want to say that those two descriptions, 'It's going to be me' and 'It's going to be someone who is merely exactly like me', don't describe different outcomes, different courses of events, only one of which can happen. They are two ways of describing one and the same course of events. What I mean by that perhaps could be shown if we take an exactly comparable case involving not a person but something about which I think we're not inclined to have a false view.

VESEY Yes.

PARFIT Something like a club. Suppose there's some club in the nineteenth century . . .

VESEY The Sherlock Holmes Club or something like that?

PARFIT Yes, perhaps. And after several years of meeting it ceases to meet. The club dies.

VESEY Right.

PARFIT And then two of its members, let's say, have emigrated to America, and after about fifteen years they get together and they start up a club. It has exactly the same rules, completely new membership except for the first two people, and they give it the same name. Now suppose someone came along and said: 'There's a real mystery here, because the following question is one that must have an answer. But how can we answer it?' The question is, 'Have they started up the very same club – is it the same club as the one they belonged to in England – or is it a completely new club that's just exactly similar?'

VESEY Yes.

PARFIT Well, in that case we all think that this man's remark is absurd; there's no difference at all. Now that's my model for the true view about the case where they make a duplicate of me. It seems that there's all the difference in the world between its being me and its being this other person who's exactly like me. But if we think there's no difference at all in the case of the clubs, why do we think there's a difference in the case of personal identity, and how can we defend the view that there's a difference?

VESEY I can see how some people would defend it. I mean, a dualist would defend it in terms of a soul being a simple thing, but . . .

PARFIT Let me try another case which I think helps to ease us out of this belief we're very strongly inclined to hold.

VESEY Go on.

PARFIT Well, this isn't a single case, this is a whole range of cases. A whole smooth spectrum of different cases which are all very similar to the next one in the range. At the start of this range of cases you suppose that the scientists are going to replace one per cent of the cells in your brain and body with exact duplicates.

VESEY Yes.

PARFIT Now if that were to be done, no one has any doubt that you'd survive. I think that's obvious because after all you can *lose* one per cent of the cells and survive. As we get further along the range they replace a larger and larger percentage of cells with exact duplicates, and of course at the far end of this range, where they replace a hundred per cent, then we've got my case where they just make a duplicate out of wholly fresh matter.

VESEY Yes.

PARFIT Now on the view that there's all the difference in the world between its being me and its being this other person who is exactly like me, we ought in consistency to think that in some case in the middle of that range, where, say, they're going to replace fifty per cent, the same question arises: is it going to be me or this completely different character? I think that even the most convinced dualist who believes in the soul is going to find this range of cases very embarrassing, because he seems committed to the view that there's some crucial percentage up to which it's going to be him and after which it suddenly ceases to be him. But I find that wholly unbelievable.

VESEY Yes. He's going to have to invent some sort of theory about the relation of mind and body to get round this one. I'm not quite sure how he would do it. Derek, could we go on to a related question? Suppose that I accepted what you said, that is, that there isn't anything more to identity than what you call psychological continuity in a one-one case. Suppose I accept that, then I would want to go on and ask you, well, what's the philosophical importance of this?

PARFIT The philosophical importance is, I think, that psychological continuity is obviously, when we think about it, a matter of degree. So long as we think that identity is a further fact, one of the things we're inclined to think is that it's all or nothing, as you said earlier. Well, if we give up that belief and if we realize that what matters in my continued existence is a matter of degree, then this does make a difference in actual cases. All the cases that I've considered so far are of course bizarre science fiction cases. But I think that in actual life it's obvious on reflection that, to give an example, the relations between me now and me next year are much closer in every way than the relations between me now and me in twenty years. And the sorts of relations that I'm thinking of are relations of memory, character, ambition, intention – all of those. Next year I shall remember much more of this year than I will in twenty years. I shall have a much more similar character. I shall be carrying out more of the same plans, ambitions and, if that is so, I think there are various plausible implications for our moral beliefs and various possible effects on our emotions.

VESEY For our moral beliefs? What have you in mind?

PARFIT Let's take one very simple example. On the view which I'm sketching it seems to me much more plausible to claim that people deserve much less punishment, or even perhaps no punishment, for what they did many years ago as compared with what they did very recently. Plausible because the relations between them now and them many years ago when they committed the crime are so much weaker.

VESEY But they are still the people who are responsible for the crime.

PARFIT I think you say that because even if they've changed in many ways, after all it was just as much they who committed the crime. I think that's true, but on the view for which I'm arguing, we would come to think that it's a completely trivial truth. It's like the following truth: it's like the truth that all of my relatives are just as much my relatives. Suppose I in my will left more money to my close relatives and less to my distant relatives; a mere pittance to my second cousin twenty-nine times removed. If you said, 'But that's clearly unreasonable because all of your relatives are just as much your relatives', there's a sense in which that's true but it's obviously too trivial to make my will an unreasonable will. And that's because what's involved in kinship is a matter of degree.

VESEY Yes.

PARFIT Now, if we think that what's involved in its being the same person now as the person who committed the crime is a matter of degree, then the truth that it was just as much him who committed the crime, will seem to us trivial in the way in which the truth that all my relatives are equally my relatives is trivial.

VESEY Yes. So you think that I should regard myself in twenty years' time as like a fairly distant relative of myself?

PARFIT Well, I don't want to exaggerate; I think the connections are much closer.

VESEY Suppose I said that this point about psychological continuity being a matter of degree – suppose I said that this isn't anything that anybody denies?

PARFIT I don't think anybody does on reflection deny that psychological continuity is a matter of degree. But I think what they may deny, and I think what may make a difference to their view, if they come over to the view for which I'm arguing – what they may deny is that psychological continuity is all there is to identity. Because what I'm arguing against is this further belief which I think we're all inclined to hold even if we don't realize it. The belief that however much we change, there's a profound sense in which the changed us is going to be just as much us. That even if some magic wand turned me into a completely different sort of person – a prince with totally different character, mental powers – it would be just as much me. That's what I'm denying.

VESEY Yes. This is the belief which I began by stating, and I think that if we did lose that belief that would be a change indeed.

PERSONAL IDENTITY AND PSYCHOLOGICAL CONTINUITY

The discussion I had with Parfit was very much a one-sided affair. The object was for him to make reasonably clear what his views are, and my job was to feed him the right questions. There was no more than a hint ('*Suppose* that

I accepted what you said . . .' etc.) that I had some reservations about his argument.

Let us reconsider what he calls 'a secular version of the Resurrection'. Suppose scientists do as Parfit suggests. That is, they 'map the states of all the cells in my brain and body' and construct 'a perfect duplicate of me out of organic matter'. But suppose they do it while I am still alive. Certainly people might mistake the duplicate for me, just as they sometimes mistake identical twins for one another. But there is nothing in this to tempt *me* to say that I am identical with the duplicate, any more than there is a temptation to say that identical twins are numerically identical. Suppose, next, that I die. We shall then have a case of one-one psychological continuity (me before death being psychologically continuous with my duplicate after my death). By Parfit's reckoning my duplicate will then qualify for the description of being identical with me. But why should the fact of my having died mean that someone who, prior to my death, was not me should now be me? Does not the idea that my duplicate becomes me on my death contradict what we ordinarily mean by personal identity?

The crucial question is: what *do* we ordinarily mean by personal identity? Is there just one thing we mean?

Wittgenstein writes:

> Our actual use of the phrase 'the same person' and of the name of a person is based on the fact that many characteristics which we use as the criteria for identity coincide in the vast majority of cases. . . . This can best be seen by imagining unreal cases which show us what different 'geometries' we would be inclined to use if facts were different. . . . Imagine a man whose memories on the even days of his life comprise the events of all these days, skipping entirely what happened on the odd days. On the other hand, he remembers on an odd day what happened on previous odd days, but his memory then skips the even days without a feeling of discontinuity. If we like we can also assume that he has alternating appearances and characteristics on odd and even days. Are we bound to say that here two persons are inhabiting the same body? That is, is it right to say that there are, and wrong to say that there aren't, or vice versa? Neither. For the *ordinary* use of the word 'person' is what one might call a composite use suitable under the ordinary circumstances. If I assume, as I do, that these circumstances are changed, the application of the term 'person' or 'personality' has thereby changed; and if I wish to preserve this term and give it a use analogous to its former use, I am at liberty to choose between many uses, that is, between many different kinds of analogy. One might say in such a case that the term 'personality' hasn't got one legitimate heir only.[1]

[1] Wittgenstein (1958) pp. 61–2.

What Wittgenstein says enables us to see why we can be led to say that a duplicate of me is, or is not, me. It depends on which of the 'many characteristics which we use as the criteria for identity' is uppermost in our minds when we consider the case. Recognition that 'the *ordinary* use of the word "person" is what one might call a composite use suitable under the ordinary circumstances' enables us to deal with the problem cases in another way than that of saying that the duplicate is, or is not, me. We can say: the question cannot be answered in terms of the ordinary use of the phrase 'the same person'.

But does not Parfit say as much? He does. He says that we can imagine cases in which the question 'Will that future person be me?' is a question which does not have any answer. But he also says that the belief most of us have about personal identity – that whatever happens between now and some future time either I shall still exist or I shall not – is false. It is this last way of putting it, in terms of *belief*, that is confusing. It is confusing because we expect questions about belief to be ones *employing* concepts rather than ones *about* concepts. Whereas the question 'In these changed circumstances would our ordinary concept of personal identity still be applicable?' is obviously a question *about* a concept, the question 'If this were to happen is it true that I would either exist or not?' has the appearance of being a question *employing* the concept.

If one mistook the question about the concept for one employing the concept then one would be likely to think of whatever concept one adopted to fit the changed circumstances as being the original concept and not a new one, one of its 'heirs'. I am prepared to accept that the concept of 'one-one psychological continuity' is one of the heirs of our ordinary concept of personal identity. Another heir would be that of bodily continuity. The point is that, as Wittgenstein puts it, 'the term "personality" hasn't got one legitimate heir only'. Parfit, I feel, gives the impression that it has one legitimate heir only.

There is a reference in the last part of our discussion to the implications of Parfit's views for our moral beliefs. These are interestingly developed in a paper he has written, 'Later Selves and Moral Principles'.[1] Two other philosophers with a special interest in personal identity are Sydney Shoemaker, from whose book *Self-Knowledge and Self-Identity*[2] I quoted earlier, and Bernard Williams, whose book is entitled *Problems of the Self*.[3]

[1] Parfit (1973).
[2] Shoemaker (1963).
[3] Williams (1973).

CHAPTER SIX

The Princess and the Philosopher

IS THERE LIFE AFTER DEATH ?

In the synopsis of his *Meditations on First Philosophy* (1641) René Descartes (1596–1650) wrote:

> What I have said is sufficient to show clearly enough that the extinction of the mind does not follow from the corruption of the body, and also to give men the hope of another life after death.[1]

In order to 'show clearly enough' that there can be life after death Descartes did not have recourse to the alleged discoveries of spiritualists. He did not attend seances, or anything like that. What he did was to shut himself up and *think*. He thought about what he could, and could not, possibly doubt. He could not possibly doubt that he was thinking, and therefore that he existed. Even an all-powerful deceiver could not have deluded him about his own existence. But such a deceiver, he thought, might well have deluded him about everything bodily. There was nothing in the indubitable fact of his thinking to guarantee that he even had a body. He could think of himself as a purely mental being. And surely it could not be beyond God's power to have created him as a purely mental being. But in that case his mind and his body are really distinct, even if they happen to be united in this earthly life. But if they are really distinct then one of them, the mind, can continue to exist when the other, the body, is dead and buried.

The conclusion was attractive, and the argument not an easy one to show to be invalid. But the doctrine that man is two distinct things, a purely spiritual soul on the one hand and a purely physical body on the other, had its difficulties. Chief among them was that of understanding how the two different 'substances' can act on one another. How can what does not take up space, the purely spiritual soul, *move* the body, as, in Descartes's view, it must when people make voluntary movements? And how can a 'cerebral motion',

---

[1] Haldane and Ross (1934) Vol. I, p. 141.

as Descartes calls it, produce a sensation in the mind, as, in his view, it must when people perceive things?

Descartes welcomed criticisms of his work. Some were from his fellow philosophers, men with established reputations and widely known views, like Thomas Hobbes (1588–1679) and Antoine Arnauld (1612–1694). Their objections to his *Meditations*, and Descartes's replies, were published along with the *Meditations*. But other exchanges were not published in his lifetime. One such was his lengthy correspondence with the Princess Elizabeth of Bohemia, daughter of the Elector Frederick, against whom Descartes had once soldiered. Descartes corresponded with her from 1643 until his death, and the work in which he gave his fullest account of the relationship between soul and body, *The Passions of the Soul* (1649), was originally composed for her.

In a letter to Elizabeth dated 28th June 1643 Descartes made what might seem to be a remarkable concession. Elizabeth had written that she found it hard to understand how the soul, if it is purely spiritual, can bring about a change in the body. She could imagine much more easily that the soul has matter and takes up space – has what philosophers call 'extension' – than that, being immaterial, it could move a body, and be affected by changes in it. Descartes replied:

> Your Highness makes the remark that it is easier to ascribe matter and extension to the soul than to ascribe to it the power of moving a body and being moved by it without having any matter. Now I would ask your Highness to hold yourself free to ascribe 'matter and extension' to the soul; . . .[1]

Could Descartes really have meant this? Could he really have meant to make a concession so damaging to his professed view, which is that the soul is distinct from the body precisely in *not* being a material thing?

The dialogue that follows answers this question. I imagined a meeting between Descartes, the philosopher, and Elizabeth, the princess, and based their discussion on the letters they wrote to one another in the 1640s. Some licence has been taken. Not all the arguments attributed to Elizabeth are to be found in her letters to Descartes. The use of a geometrical example towards the end of the dialogue, in particular, comes not from the Descartes–Elizabeth correspondence, but from the objections made to the *Meditations* by Antoine Arnauld.[2] But an effort has been made not to introduce philosophical ideas of later centuries.

[1] Anscombe and Geach (1954) p. 281.

[2] Haldane and Ross (1934) Vol. II, pp. 83–5. Descartes's reply to the argument based on the geometrical example is to be found on pp. 100–2 of the same volume.

THE PRINCESS AND THE PHILOSOPHER

[*Conversation and music in a large hall*]

DESCARTES ... Madame, the honour that your Highness does in greeting me is greater than I dared to hope. It is most consoling not only to receive the favour of your commandments in writing, but to encounter you.

ELIZABETH You are welcome, Master. Your letters have given me much pleasure.

DESCARTES I am most obliged to your Highness for reading them. Even when you see how badly I explain myself, you still have patience to hear me. [*Slight pause*] But tell me, Madame, how can I help you and what subjects still bemuse your Highness? When I read the traces of your thought on paper, I find a truly amazing comprehension of the abstract matters on which I write. But now, seeing before me a body such as painters give to angels from which these superhuman sentiments flow, I am ravished like a man come fresh to heaven. Anything you ask, I will answer, if I can.

ELIZABETH Let us move to a quieter room.
[*They move to a quiet room and sit down*]

ELIZABETH I wrote to you, you will remember, about the nature of the soul. I asked you how the soul, if it is an immaterial thing, can move the body. Surely, if one object is to move another, the first must be in physical contact with the second. I cannot play my harpsichord without touching the keys with my fingers. How can the soul, if it is purely spiritual, touch the body to bring about changes in it?

DESCARTES Forgive me, Madame, I answered that question, did I not?

ELIZABETH You replied to my letter, but I don't think you answered my question. You wrote that people suppose heaviness to be something that moves objects, and yet moves them without their being touched. Heaviness makes the leaves fall to the ground and this is obviously different from the way that one ball, when it strikes another, makes it move. In other words – and this I took to be your point – we do have a notion of one thing moving another without making contact with it.

DESCARTES Ah ... so you agree with me.

ELIZABETH [*Slight pause – continues puzzled*] But the way in which heaviness moves the leaves is very different from the way the soul moves the body. Heaviness is not immaterial in the way that, according to you, the soul is immaterial. It isn't – how shall I put it? – heaviness isn't a *mental* force.

What I can't understand is how a thought can bring about a bodily movement. You aren't saying that it does so by heaviness, are you? In any case, I don't know what that means.

DESCARTES No, no, no, no, no. My point is that we do have a notion of things being moved without other things making physical contact with them. [*Slight pause*] As a matter of fact, this notion is misapplied when we use it to understand why things fall to the ground. In my *Physics* I showed that the heaviness of things is not, in fact, something distinct from them. But we do have this notion and I believe we were given it in order to understand how the soul moves the body. If, by using this notion, we can understand how the soul moves the body, we can also see how a man's soul and body are united.

ELIZABETH But all the emphasis, in your *Meditations*, is on their being distinct.

DESCARTES Yes, but there are two things to remember about the soul. First, it is a thing which thinks. Second, it is united to the body, and so can act and suffer along with it. I said almost nothing about the second in my *Meditations*. My aim there was to show that the soul is distinct from the body, and it would only have confused matters to have said, at the same time, that they are united.

ELIZABETH [*Interrupting*] Oh yes, but now you must explain. Because if you simply say that the soul and body are united, and leave it at that, I'm really no better off. How can what is spiritual be united with what is corporeal, physical, material, 'extended'? Master, I accept that soul and body are united, but if I am to understand how the soul can act on the body, I must understand the principle of their union. How are soul and body, two distinct substances, united?

DESCARTES [*Pensively*] Well, it isn't by the intellect, with which we comprehend the soul, that we can also understand the union of soul and body. Nor is it by the intellect aided by the imagination. That leaves only the senses. So it is through the senses that we understand the union of soul and body. When we philosophize on these matters we realize that soul and body are distinct; but so far as our experience is concerned it's as if they were one. When I raise my arm, or have a pain in my back, I don't feel myself to be separate from my arm or my back. But I know, nevertheless, that my soul is distinct from my body.

ELIZABETH You are saying that it *feels* as if body and soul are united?

DESCARTES Indeed.

ELIZABETH But that doesn't explain *how* they are united, does it? You said we understand the union of soul and body by the senses. But knowing *that* the soul acts on the body isn't knowing how. [*Pause*] You see, it seems to me that if the soul and body do act on one another, then we ought to be able to understand how they do so. The senses don't seem to provide that sort of knowledge. [*Descartes still does not reply*] It was because I couldn't see how the immaterial soul could act on the physical body that I suggested that the soul, in its substance as distinct from its activity, must be material. If thinking, willing, and so on, are things that the *body* does, instead of things done by a spiritual thing which is distinct from the body, my problem doesn't arise.

DESCARTES But what do you mean by 'substance'? It's the soul's activities – thinking, willing, and so on – that make it the substance it is. Thought is the essence of the soul, just as 'extension' – taking up space – is the essence of matter. No substance can have two essences.

ELIZABETH [*Indignant*] Yet I clearly remember your saying in a letter that I could 'ascribe matter and extension to the soul.'

DESCARTES When was that?

ELIZABETH About three years ago, I think.

DESCARTES In what connection?

ELIZABETH I can find the letter for you. [*She rummages*] Yes, here it is. Let me find the place . . . Ah! 'Your Highness remarks that it is easier to ascribe matter and extension to the soul than to ascribe to an *im*material thing the ability to move a material thing and be moved by it. Now I would ask your Highness to feel free to ascribe matter and extension to the soul . . .'

DESCARTES Ah, but how does it go on?

ELIZABETH Er '. . . matter and extension to the soul; for this is nothing else than to conceive the soul as united to the body.'

DESCARTES [*Animated*] You see! I was still talking about the soul being united to the body. The soul is, in a sense, extended. For example, when we feel aches and pains in various parts of our bodies. . . . Suppose you prick your finger on a spindle . . .

ELIZABETH Aren't you confusing me with another Princess?

DESCARTES I said 'suppose'. Suppose you prick your finger on a spindle. You feel pain. Where do you feel the pain? In your finger. In a way it's almost as if your soul were extended throughout your body, even into your fingers. But to talk in that way is to talk only of feeling. The pain isn't really in your finger, it's in your soul. You know by your intellect that it isn't in your finger, since you know by your intellect that the soul, which suffers pain, is immaterial. To know the truth of the matter we must trust the intellect.

ELIZABETH The intellect, you say, tells us that the soul is immaterial. But is our intellectual perception of the soul sufficiently clear? Perhaps if we had a clearer perception of its nature we would realize that it is, in fact, material. Isn't there at least this possibility?

DESCARTES Not if the argument of my *Meditations* is sound. You remember, I imagined that an extremely powerful, malicious demon does everything he can to deceive us?

ELIZABETH Yes.

DESCARTES He may deceive me about everything that has to do with my body, but when it comes to my thinking – well, then he can't deceive me. That I cannot doubt. [*Slowly and emphatically*] Therefore, in so far as I cannot be deceived about my existence I am no more than a thinking thing.

ELIZABETH Agreed. But that is 'what you cannot be deceived about'. The question I'm raising is a different one. It isn't about what you do or don't know; it's about what is in fact the case. I'm suggesting that although you can suppose yourself not to have bodily attributes it may nevertheless be the case that you do have them.

DESCARTES No. They may seem quite different questions – the one about what I know or don't know and the one about what is in fact the case – but they aren't. They're connected.

ELIZABETH How? How are they connected?

DESCARTES Well, it's really to do with possibilities. If it is possible for thinking to go on apart from a body then . . .

ELIZABETH [*Interrupting*] But *is* it possible? That's the question.

DESCARTES All right, I'm coming to that. I did say 'if'. If it is possible for thinking, and the body, to exist in separation then . . .

ELIZABETH [*Impatiently*] Yes, yes, then what-does-the-thinking isn't the body. I can quite see that. But what you've got to do is to get rid of the 'if'. That is, you've got to show it to be possible for thinking to go on apart from a body.

DESCARTES Precisely, and that is where what I know and don't know, comes in.

ELIZABETH Go on.

DESCARTES Well, I know certainly that I am thinking and at the same time I can doubt that I have bodily attributes. So I can perceive the one thing, the thinking, apart from the other. And since this perception is clear and distinct it must be possible for the one thing to exist apart from the other.

ELIZABETH Just a moment. You said 'since this perception is clear and distinct'.

DESCARTES Yes.

ELIZABETH And you'd say that if you clearly and distinctly perceive yourself as no more than a thinking thing then it would follow that you could exist as no more than a thinking thing?

DESCARTES Yes.

ELIZABETH And therefore that you really are no more than a thinking thing?

DESCARTES Exactly.

ELIZABETH All right. Well now, isn't it possible that your perception is clear, but only as far as it goes? And that it doesn't go far enough for you to know the truth? In other words, isn't it possible that you really do have bodily properties although your knowledge of yourself doesn't go beyond your mental properties?

DESCARTES No. You must distinguish between clearness and completeness. Certainly there may be things about me which I haven't clearly perceived. But that doesn't affect what I have clearly perceived. And, having clearly perceived that I am a thinking thing, I know that I can exist as such. That is, I know that what I am certain of – my intellectual faculty – is enough for me to exist with. And if it is enough for me to exist with, then I really am distinct from anything bodily.

ELIZABETH So, the principle of your argument is: if I can clearly perceive something to be such-and-such while I cannot clearly perceive it to be so-and-so, then it can exist simply as such-and-such.

DESCARTES Yes.

ELIZABETH But now, consider this case. A triangle is a plane figure bounded by three straight lines.

DESCARTES Mm.

ELIZABETH That is something most people know. But not everyone knows that the angles of a triangle add up to two right angles. That is, someone might know very well that something was a triangle, and yet not know this further fact about its angles. Now, on your reasoning it should be possible for there to be a triangle whose angles did not add up to two right angles. Do you see what I mean?

DESCARTES Yes, it's the same point as Father Arnauld made in the fourth set of objections to my *Meditations*. But I do not accept that they are parallel cases. And I say why in my answer to him.

ELIZABETH I'll have to look at that again. [*Pause*] You see, it isn't that I don't want to believe you. Unless you are right about the soul being distinct from the body, I don't see how there can be any hope of life after death. If it is some part of my body that thinks and wills, then when it decays in death there is an end of me. On your view, moreover, God has made man in his likeness. Only if we perceive ourselves to be purely spiritual can we think of God likewise. These thoughts are precious to me, Master Descartes. I accept them as a matter of faith, but I would that faith and reason should go together. [*Sighs*] The soul grows weary of its burdensome shroud of flesh. There are times when I long to be released from it to a happier life above.

DESCARTES Madame, I know of the exile that threatens you, and I grieve that there is nothing I can do to help.

ELIZABETH But there is, Master Descartes. There is. Your letters are a great comfort to me and I hope you'll continue to write. Thus shall the months seem weeks, and the weeks days.

DESCARTES I wish I could be of more material service to you. I wish . . .

ELIZABETH [*Interrupting*] Go now, good master. Go out and make free of the court which has banished me. Turn their hearts and minds to philosophy as you have turned mine. It is their evil that I must bear. Moderate it if you can . . .

EXORCISING THE GHOST IN THE MACHINE

Two questions that Princess Elizabeth asks, in the dialogue, are (i) Is our intellectual perception of the soul sufficiently clear for us to know that it is immaterial? and (ii) If the soul *is* immaterial, how can it act on the body? Both these questions received considerable attention from philosophers writing after Descartes. The British empiricist philosopher John Locke (1632–1704) gave a negative answer to the first. Our idea of spiritual substance, he said, is an idea of 'a supposed I know not what' that 'supports' thinking and willing ('the power of putting body into motion by thought'). Similarly, our idea of material substance is an idea of something about which we know nothing except that it 'supports' solidity and 'the power of communicating motion by impulse'. This being so, we cannot know that the 'support' of thinking is not the same thing as the 'support' of solidity,

> it being impossible for us, by the contemplation of our own ideas without revelation, to discover whether Omnipotency has not given to some systems of matter, fitly disposed, a power to perceive and think, . . . it being, in respect of our notions, not much more remote from our comprehension to conceive that God can, if He pleases, superadd to matter a faculty of thinking, than that he should superadd to it another substance with a faculty of thinking; since we know not wherein thinking consists, nor to what sort of substances the Almighty has been pleased to give that power . . .[1]

Descartes, of course, thought he had proved that it is an immaterial substance that thinks, and not, as we would ordinarily say, a person; still less, the 'system of matter' which is a person's brain. Princess Elizabeth's doubts about his argument have been succinctly expressed by A. M. MacIver:

> Descartes tried to prove demonstratively that what thinks in us must be unextended, starting from the *Cogito*.[2] I know that I exist, because I think, and I know this with certainty; but, in knowing myself to exist, I do not know myself to be extended, because, while sure of my own existence, I can still be doubtful of the existence of all bodies; it is therefore concluded that the 'I' which is certainly known to exist is a thinking thing but not an extended thing – or in other words, an immaterial mind. This argument, with its professed conclusion, depends on the simple fallacy of supposing that, if we do not know with certainty that something is the case, we certainly know that it is not the case: if I know that I exist but do not know whether or not I am extended, I know that I am not extended.[3]

MacIver points out that Descartes's conclusion is at odds with our everyday way of talking:

> If we accept the Platonic and Cartesian account of human nature, we ought strictly to say '*I* think' but '*My body* sits' and '*My body* walks', and if this account came naturally to men, this (or something which made the same distinction) would be normal colloquial usage; but in fact, ordinary language says equally '*I*

[1] Pringle–Pattison (1924) pp. 268–70.

[2] *Cogito* (Latin) = I think.

[3] MacIver (1936) p. 101.

think', '*I* sit', '*I* walk' – implying that *prima facie* the subject is in each case the same.[1]

The view that there is one subject, namely a *person*, such that *both* predicates like 'think' *and* predicates like 'walk' are equally applicable to it is one for which P. F. Strawson has argued in his book *Individuals*[2]. A crucial step in the argument is 'that a necessary condition of states of consciousness being ascribed at all is that they should be ascribed to the *very same things* as certain corporeal characteristics, a certain physical situation, etc.'[3]

MacIver holds that Descartes's real reason for believing that the subject that thinks is not extended was not the one he gave in the *Cogito* argument. He holds that Descartes's real reason was his belief that the behaviour of extended things could be explained mechanically, and that since thought is obviously not a mechanical process it could not be an extended thing that thinks.[4]

Gilbert Ryle, in *The Concept of Mind*, endorses MacIver's explanation of how Descartes really came to believe in an unextended substance:

> When Galileo showed that his methods of scientific discovery were competent to provide a mechanical theory which should cover every occupant of space, Descartes found in himself two conflicting motives. As a man of scientific genius he could not but endorse the claims of mechanics, yet as a religious and moral man he could not accept, as Hobbes accepted, the discouraging rider to those claims, namely that human nature differs only in degree of complexity from clockwork. The mental could not be just a variety of the mechanical.
>
> He and subsequent philosophers naturally but erroneously availed themselves of the following escape-route. Since mental-conduct words are not to be construed as signifying the occurrence of mechanical processes, they must be construed as signifying the occurrence of non-mechanical processes; . . . so, while some movements of human tongues and limbs are the effects of mechanical causes, others must be the effects of non-mechanical causes, i.e. some issue from movements of particles of matter, others from workings of the mind.[5]

One of the major difficulties in accepting this 'non-mechanical-causes' view is the one to which Princess Elizabeth gave expression, that of explaining how immaterial minds can bring about changes in material bodies.

[1] Ibid., p. 99.

[2] Strawson (1964) Chapter 3.

[3] Ibid., p. 102.

[4] MacIver, *ibid.*, p. 102.

[5] Ryle (1963) p. 20.

There are two ways of responding to a philosophical problem like this. One is to accept the terms in which it is formulated, and try to answer it in those terms. The other is to repudiate the terms; that is, to show that some sort of mistake has been made in the setting-up of the problem. Ryle adopts the second of these courses. He says that a 'category mistake' had been made in representing the differences between the physical and the mental as 'differences inside the common framework of the categories of "thing", "stuff", "attribute", "state", "process", "change", "cause", and "effect"'.[1]

To accept the terms in which the problem has been posed is to try to answer the question 'If the soul *is* immaterial, how can it act on the body?' One philosopher who tries to answer this question is Nicolas Malebranche (1638–1715). Malebranche's answer is given, and discussed, in Chapter Seven of this book.

If the terms in which the problem has been set are repudiated then there will nevertheless remain a question, of some sort, that requires an answer. In this case it is the question: 'If a voluntary action is *not* to be understood as a bodily motion caused by an act of "will", how *is* it to be understood?' An answer to this question is suggested in Chapter Eight of this book. See also Chapter Two.

There are relevant extracts from the writings of Descartes (including some of his correspondence with Princess Elizabeth), Locke, MacIver, Strawson, Ryle and Malebranche in *Body and Mind*, edited by G. N. A. Vesey. This is a collection of extracts from the writings of forty-one philosophers from Descartes onwards, on the problem of the relation of body and mind.

[1] Ibid.

CHAPTER SEVEN

Body and Mind, United

HOW ARE BODY AND MIND UNITED ?

In Chapter Six I said that the chief difficulty in Descartes's doctrine that man is two distinct things is understanding how they can act on one another. Descartes's own explanation of mind-body interaction was in terms of two notions: (i) that the soul is united to the body, and (ii) that it is 'ordained by Nature', or happens 'naturally', that certain mental events should accompany certain bodily events, and vice versa.[1]

This raises two questions: (a) What can it mean to talk of two distinct substances being 'united'? and (b) What are we to understand by the reference to 'Nature'? It will be apparent from the dialogue in Chapter Six that Princess Elizabeth did not find Descartes's notion of the union of soul and body of much explanatory value. Nor did Nicolas Malebranche (1638–1715). In his *Metaphysical and Religious Conversations* he put into the mouth of Aristes views very like those of Descartes:

> I believe that God has united my mind to my body so that in consequence of this union my mind and my body can act reciprocally upon one another, in virtue of the natural laws which God always follows very closely.[2]

Then, as Theodore, he commented:

> This word 'union' explains nothing. It is itself in need of explanation. Thus, Aristes, you may like to take vague and general words for reasons. But do not think you can pay us in this coin, for though many people accept it and are satisfied with it, we are not so easily dealt with.[3]

Malebranche himself supplied the explanation which he thought the word 'union' needed. He did so by bringing in God.

---

[1] Anscombe and Geach (1954) p. 246 and Haldane and Ross (1934) Vol. 1, pp. 350–1.

[2] Malebranche (1923) p. 181.

[3] Ibid., p. 183.

It is clear that, in the union of soul and body, there is no other bond than the efficacy of divine and immutable decrees.[1]

It is God alone who produces in your soul all those different feelings which it experiences, on the occasion of the changes which take place in your body, in consequence of the general laws of the conjunction of the two natures of which man is constituted; laws which are nothing but the efficient and constant volitions of the creator.[2]

The dialogue that follows is adapted from Malebranche's *Metaphysical and Religious Conversations* by Oswald Hanfling, Lecturer in Philosophy at The Open University. I have retained his introduction, his comment half-way through the dialogue, and his conclusion.

BODY AND MIND: A DIALOGUE FROM MALEBRANCHE

HANFLING In 1688 the French philosopher Nicolas Malebranche published his *Metaphysical and Religious Conversations*. Although his writing is full of echoes from Augustine and Plato, Malebranche is known chiefly for his development of Descartes's philosophy of body and mind. In the *Conversations* Malebranche states the Cartesian position with great persuasiveness and tries to solve one of the main problems to which it gave rise. This is the problem of how the interaction of mind and body is to be conceived. The *Conversations* are enlivened by many witty and ironical exchanges, but the philosopher never loses sight of the underlying seriousness of his problem, which, after all, concerns nothing less than the essential nature of man. And what Malebranche had to say about that problem retains its interest and relevance for anyone seriously concerned about it today.

The main participants in the *Conversations* are two imaginary characters called Theodore and Aristes. On the whole Theodore is Malebranche's mouthpiece, but as you will hear, Aristes is by no means a mere stooge; he gives forceful expression to alternative views and possible objections to what is maintained by Theodore; and from time to time he brings the conversation down to earth when his partner's enthusiasm threatens to outsoar the reader's comprehension. In my adaptation I have tried to bring out both the flavour of Malebranche's style and the cogency of his argument.

[1] Ibid., p. 130.

[2] Ibid., p. 165.

THEODORE Well, my dear Aristes, since you want it, I shall have to talk to you about my metaphysical visions. But for this purpose I must leave this enchanting place, which charms our senses, and is too diverting for a mind like mine. Let us go and shut ourselves up in your study, so that nothing will prevent us from consulting our master, universal reason. It is inner truth that must preside over our discussions.

ARISTES Let us go, Theodore, anywhere you wish. I am disgusted with all that I see in this material world, ever since I heard you talk of another world which is full of *intelligible* beauty. Take me to that happy and enchanted region. Come, I'm ready to follow you to that country . . .

THEODORE [*Deflated*] You are making fun, Aristes. But I'm not angry.

ARISTES Theodore, I . . .

THEODORE I forgive you. But don't mind my telling you, you're talking about something you don't understand. No, I shall not take you to a strange land; but I shall perhaps teach you that you are a stranger in your own country. I shall teach you that this world which you inhabit is not at all what you think it is. You judge your environment by what you learn from your senses, but your senses deceive you far more than you can imagine.

ARISTES You took what I said too seriously, Theodore. I promise you . . .

THEODORE You didn't make me angry, Aristes. I was pleased by your lively imagination. You will never make me angry, and you'll always give me pleasure – so long as you make fun of me only when we are alone.

ARISTES Let us go quickly then, Theodore. . . . Come in and take a seat. I'll draw the curtains. Now nothing can prevent us from reflecting inwardly and consulting our reason.

THEODORE Now, Aristes. Reject all that has entered your mind by way of the senses. Try to forget even that you have a body. The only thing I ask for is your attention. Without this, without pitting your mind against the impressions of the body, you won't make any conquests in the land of truth.

ARISTES I'm ready, Theodore. But allow me to stop you if I can't follow.

THEODORE Agreed. Now listen. *I think, therefore I am.* But what am I – I who think – during the time that I think? Am I a body, a mind, a man? All I know is that during the time that I think I am something that thinks. But let's see. Can a *body* think? Can it reason, desire, feel? No, surely. So the 'I' that thinks, is not a body. A body has extension, it has length, width and depth. But it's evident that my thoughts, my feelings and desires don't have extension. They can't be measured. So my soul is not material; it's a substance which thinks, and which has no resemblance whatever to the extended substance of which my body is composed.

ARISTES Yes. And what conclusions do you draw from that?

THEODORE An infinite number. But just let me say this. If the soul is a substance distinct from the body, then it's evident that even if death were to annihilate our body it wouldn't follow that our soul would be annihilated. But now let me prove some other things to you.

ARISTES Go on, I'm listening carefully.

THEODORE I think you are good at music, aren't you? I've often seen you playing musical instruments.

ARISTES Oh, I can play well enough to amuse myself.

THEODORE Well now. Explain to me the nature of the various sounds. What is an octave, a fifth, a fourth? You have a very fine and delicate ear. Consult it, so that it can tell you what I want to know.

ARISTES I think you're making fun of me. Surely it's reason, and not the senses, that must be consulted.

THEODORE That is true. The power of the senses is very limited, but reason ranges over all things. Consult it then, and be careful not to confuse its response with the testimony of your senses. Well, what does it tell you?

ARISTES You are going too fast for me. Well, it, it seems to me that sound is a quality which is spread about in the air, and which can only affect the sense of hearing.

THEODORE And is that what you call consulting reason?

ARISTES But what do you want me to say? Wait. Here is an octave: *la-la*; here is a fifth: *do-so*; here is a fourth: *do-fa*.

THEODORE You sing well, but how badly you reason! Lend me that instrument there, Aristes, and pay attention to what I am going to do and say. When I pull this string towards me and let it go again like this [*he plucks*] it produces, as you can see, a lot of vibrations. This disturbs the air surrounding it, and the disturbance is passed on to our ears – yours and mine.

ARISTES That's true. But it's a *sound* that I can hear; a sound spread through the air. And a sound is surely a different quality from vibrations and disturbances of air.

THEODORE Yes. And it's just because of that that you spoke wrongly when you said that the *sound* is spread through the air. Because – note this carefully – when I pluck this string [*he plucks*] I merely make it vibrate; and a vibrating string merely agitates the air which surrounds it.

ARISTES Merely agitates the air which surrounds it. . . . Why, don't you hear that it produces a *sound* in the air?

THEODORE Well, I hear what you hear. But when I want to find out the truth about something, I don't consult my ears, though you consult yours, in spite of the good resolutions you made. Just reflect, and consult the clear ideas of reason. Can you really conceive that air is capable of containing the sound that you hear? Think carefully. Isn't it evident that all properties of extended things must be relations of distance?

ARISTES Relations of distance?

THEODORE Yes, properties like shape and movement.

ARISTES Yes, that's evident.

THEODORE And so Aristes, the sound, which you agree to be something other than movement, is *not* spread in the air. It's a sensation, something that happens to the soul.

ARISTES Yes, I can see that.

THEODORE Can you? Well now, tell me, what is an octave, and a fifth? Or rather, teach me what one has to do in order to hear these sounds.

ARISTES Very well. Take the octave, then. In order to get the octave, you divide the string into two parts. First you pluck the whole string [*he plucks*]; then one of the two parts, to get the octave. [*He plucks*]

THEODORE And why is that so?

ARISTES Oh, it's because sound is to sound as string is to string.

THEODORE I don't quite understand that principle.

ARISTES Well, look. The string and its vibrations cause the various sounds. [*Speaks rather too quickly*] Now the whole cause is to its half as two is to one, and the effects correspond exactly to their causes. So the effect of the whole cause is double the effect of half of it: the sound of the whole string is to the sound of half of it as two is to one.

THEODORE Do you really understand what you are saying?

ARISTES Well, what objection do you find to my reasoning?

THEODORE [*Sympathetically*] There is a good deal in it. . . . But look. Let's try a little experiment. Now give me your hand – I won't hurt you. I am now rubbing the palm of your hand with my sleeve. Do you feel anything?

ARISTES Yes – a little warmth – a kind of *pleasant* feeling.

THEODORE Hm. And now?

ARISTES Ow, you're hurting me. You are rubbing too hard.

THEODORE You are mistaken, Aristes! What you really feel is a pleasant feeling – twice as pleasant as the one you felt before. Look, I can prove it to you. My rubbing of your hand is the cause of what you feel. Now, the whole cause is to its half as two is to one, and the effects correspond exactly to their causes. I rubbed twice as hard. So what you really felt . . .

ARISTES All right. I am punished for having reasoned badly. You hurt me, and then, by way of an excuse, you prove to me that you really gave me a double amount of pleasure. Is that how you teach people?

THEODORE What else can I do?

ARISTES [*Pause*] But surely, when I pluck the string, I hear the sound.

THEODORE Yes, I concede that. [*Emphatically*] But there is no relation of *causality* between a body and a mind.

ARISTES What you've been telling me, Theodore, is terribly abstract. I'm having some trouble in keeping my mind on it. Let's have a little rest, if you don't mind. I shall think at leisure about these great and important truths.

THEODORE Meditate on what I told you, and I promise that tomorrow you will be ready for everything. Goodbye, Aristes. I leave you alone with Reason.

HANFLING At this stage the argument has really got rather stuck. Two things have been proved to Aristes, both of them negative. The first is that what goes on in the mind when one hears a sound or feels a pain is not to be identified with anything physical like vibrations or rubbings.

And the second is that there is not even a relation of causality between the mental and physical. What then is the relation between them – between mind and body? This is the question that continues to trouble Aristes on the intervening day. It is pretty clear from what follows, by the way, that he's spent that day in poring over the works of Descartes.

ARISTES Where have you been, Theodore? I was getting impatient at not meeting you.

THEODORE What, isn't Reason sufficient for you, to pass your time agreeably in its company?

ARISTES I've made great progress since you left me, Theodore.

THEODORE What do you think, then, Aristes, of what we were saying yesterday?

ARISTES Well, it seems to me that there's nothing to which I am more closely united than my own body. It can't be touched without disturbing me. Take even those little insects which are such a nuisance on our evening walk. As soon as they stick their tiny needles into me, I feel a pain in my soul. If the sun did not disturb my eyes, it would be invisible for me. I really am more closely united to my body than to any other thing.

THEODORE Have you meditated long, my dear Aristes, in order to make this great discovery?

ARISTES I see I've made a bad beginning.

THEODORE Very bad indeed. I didn't think you'd forget today what you knew yesterday. Well now, I submit to you that we are not 'united' to our body at all, let alone that . . .

ARISTES But surely one is only saying what one knows when one says that the body acts on the mind. It's something we can't doubt in the face of experience.

THEODORE *I* doubt it, or rather, I don't believe it at all. Experience teaches me that I feel pain, for example, when a pin pricks me. That's certain. But experience doesn't in any way teach me that the pin *acts* on my mind.

ARISTES No . . . I wouldn't say that a pin can act on my mind. But perhaps one could say that it acts on my body – and through my body on my mind because of their union. I admit that matter can't act *immediately* on the mind. Note the word 'im-mediately'.

THEODORE But what about your body, isn't it composed of matter?

ARISTES Yes, of course.

THEODORE Then your *body* can't act 'im-mediately' on your mind. So although your finger is pricked by a pin and your brain is disturbed by this action, neither the one nor the other can act on your soul and make it feel pain. Your brain and your finger are merely matter. You say there is the closest union in the world between your mind and your body. But this word 'union' explains nothing.

ARISTES Well, what do you want me to do? Prove to me that body and soul act mutually on each other *without* having recourse to their union.

THEODORE My dear Aristes, don't keep talking about a union of soul and body: *Your soul is united only to God.* God has willed that you should have certain feelings – certain emotions – whenever there are certain disturbances in your brain. He has willed, and he wills incessantly, that what happens to the mind and to the body should be reciprocal. *That* is the union and the natural dependence of the two parts of which we are composed.

ARISTES Yes . . . I admit, Theodore, that there is an essential relation between created things and the Creator. But . . .

THEODORE And now, Aristes, you are ready to make thousands of discoveries in the land of truth. [*He gets worked up*] Lift yourself up to Reason, and you will see the light. Silence your senses, your imagination and your passions, and you will hear the pure voice of inner truth. The stronger our feelings are, the more obscurity they spread. You must follow Reason in spite of all the caresses of the body. Do you understand this clearly?

ARISTES It does strike me, Theodore, that your exhortation is rather heated for a discussion on metaphysics! You seem to be exciting my feelings, instead of giving rise to clear ideas. But to be honest, I still don't quite understand what you are telling me. One moment I see it, and the next moment . . .

HANFLING Malebranche's belief in the dualism of mind and body, and in the supremacy of the one over the other, was borne out by the manner of his death in 1715. 'His disease', says Fontenelle, 'adapted itself to his philosophy. The body, which he so much despised, was reduced to nothing; but the mind, accustomed to supremacy, continued sane and sound. He remained throughout a calm spectator of his own long death.'

ARE THE MENTAL AND THE PHYSICAL TWO ASPECTS OF THE SAME THING?

Malebranche was not the only philosopher to give a God-centred explanation of the 'union' of mind and body. G. W. Leibniz (1647–1716) did so, too, and discussed the difference between his own explanation and that of Malebranche in a letter to Antoine Arnauld dated 30 April 1687.[1]

A third philosopher who gave a God-centred explanation was Baruch Spinoza (1632–1677). Like Malebranche he aimed at providing an explanation that would enable us to 'understand not only that the human mind is united to the body, but also what must be understood by the union of the mind and the body'.[2] But unlike Malebranche's, his view of how God is related to the world is such that it is not difficult to derive a non-theocentric account of the relation of mind and body from his theocentric one. Indeed, taken out of context, one might suppose some of his remarks to be the expression of just such a non-theocentric account. In the Note to Proposition II in Part II of his *Ethics*, for instance, he says that the mind and the body are one and the same thing, which is conceived now under the attribute of thought and now under the attribute of extension. This may be clearer with an example. Suppose I have a migraine. 'Under the attribute of thought' it is a mental thing, a pain. But 'under the attribute of extension' it is something physical, perhaps a dilation of the arteries of my brain. The physical and the mental are not related as cause and effect; they are two aspects of one and the same thing.

One finds practically the same thing being said by some twentieth-century scientists. A professor of physical chemistry, J. A. V. Butler, writes:

> It is difficult to deal objectively with feelings and sensations because they are absolutely personal and private to each person. There is no way in which they can be shared with other people. You cannot see what your friend sees or feel what he feels. If he tells you he has a pain you can imagine what it feels like, but there is no conceivable way in which you can feel the pain. You merely infer from his behaviour that he has feelings like your own.
>
> My private world of perceptions and feelings is something entirely different from the outer world which I believe to exist. I can look at a scene and interpret my sense impressions of it. I see trees, houses, and perhaps people. I can analyse this picture further and notice that the trees belong to a class of things which I call plants, while the people are in many respects similar to another kind called animals. I can go further and remember that all these objects have been convinc-

---

[1] Leibniz (1967).

[2] Spinoza (1910) Part II, Proposition XIII, Note.

ingly analysed and shown to be capable of interpretation as consisting of chemical compounds which are themselves made up of atoms. All this is my interpretation of the various perceptions present in my consciousness.

The awareness itself, the mental picture which I am analysing and interpreting, cannot be discussed at all in any of the terms which are used to discuss and interpret the outer world. . . . So we find ourselves in a dilemma. Must the scientific picture of the outside world stop short of mental phenomena and leave us incapable of accounting for what we know best (indeed our only direct knowledge) – namely our own perceptions and feelings? . . .

Some scientists have met this dilemma by denying the existence of the inner world, at any rate as a subject of science. If it can never be approached scientifically, they say, we might as well ignore it. It does not exist scientifically. . . . We must be content to describe the surges of impulses in the brain. For the scientist this *is* the sensation. The fact that I am *aware* of something does not concern him.

If we are not willing to ignore the inner world of perception, but think we must accept it as real – at least as real as the outer world which we have inferred – we must admit that, although consciousness cannot be described in the same terms as the 'matter' of the outside world, it is curiously associated with it and all our conscious states seem to have some physical background or equivalent. This intimate association of the two worlds (the inner world of experience and the outer world of matter) suggests that they may only be two distinct aspects of a single phenomenon.[1]

This may seem less far-fetched than Malebranche's theocentric view but it leaves unanswered the awkward question 'What is the thing – the "single phenomenon" as Butler calls it – of which the mental and the physical are the two aspects?' It may be argued that if we cannot answer that question then we have not really made any progress in our understanding of the relation of mind and matter.[2]

In the absence of any notion of some third thing that is, in itself, neither mental nor physical, but presents mental and physical appearances, there is a temptation to say that the brain is the thing that presents the appearances: sensations and feelings are how what happens in the brain appears to the person whose brain it is. This is a view which has its roots in behaviourist psychology, or, rather, in the attempts of behaviourist psychologists to say something about sensations. Psychologists like E. C. Tolman and E. G.

[1] Butler (1954) pp. 98–100.

[2] Pearson (1900) p. 48: 'It is no use, indeed it is only dangerous, in the present state of our knowledge with regard to psychology and the physics of the brain, to fill the void of ignorance by hypotheses which can neither be proved nor refuted. Thus if we say that thought and motion are the same thing seen from different sides, we make no real progress in our analysis for we can form no conception whatever as to what the nature in itself of this thing may be.'

Boring, in the United States, and C. S. Myers, in Britain, writing in the 1930s toyed with various versions of this theory. The philosopher Roy Wood Sellars, in his book *The Philosophy of Physical Realism*, came close to advocating the theory. He wrote:

> Consciousness is the qualitative dimension of a brain-event. It is the patterned brain event as sentient. It is because of its status that we, as conscious, participate in the being of brain-events. Here, and here alone, are we, as conscious beings, on the inside of reality.[1]

The phrase 'on the inside of reality' has a lovely ring to it, but can hardly be held to explain what is meant by 'the qualitative dimension of a brain-event'. Use of the less metaphorical-sounding word 'identity' does not help. The statement 'Sensations are identical with brain processes' is not like, say, 'Flashes of lightning are identical with electrical discharges'. The first is about a whole category of being, the latter is not. A closer parallel would be: 'Things in the ordinarily accepted world of everyday experience are identical with things in the world of the physical sciences.' But if 'Sensations are identical with brain processes' is like 'Things in the ordinarily accepted world of everyday experience are identical with things in the world of the physical sciences' then what is its status? Is it advanced as a scientific theory? (If so, what would falsify it?) Or as a methodological postulate; that is, something we must assume in order to do physiological psychology? (If so, why would not a statement of isomorphism – that is, that there is a brain-state corresponding to every mental state – serve as well?)

If you want to follow up these issues I recommend the papers by J. J. C. Smart, 'Sensations and Brain Processes', and Jerome Shaffer, 'Could mental states be brain processes?' in *Body and Mind*, edited by G. N. A. Vesey.

[1] Sellars (1932) p. 414.

CHAPTER EIGHT

Sensation and Interpretation in Perception

IMPLICATIONS OF THE MIND-BODY RELATIONSHIP BEING CAUSAL

Princess Elizabeth's doubts about Descartes's account of voluntary action took the form of puzzlement as to how 'an immaterial being has the capacity of moving a body'.[1] It was this problem which Descartes tried to solve by reference to 'the union of soul and body'.[2] And it was to elucidating the concept of 'the union of soul and body' that the efforts of Malebranche, Leibniz, and Spinoza were directed. All five of them – Descartes, Princess Elizabeth, Malebranche, Leibniz and Spinoza – saw the issue as being one of explaining how something mental, a 'volition', can bring about something physical, a change in the state of the brain. Descartes wrote:

> The action of the soul consists entirely in this, that, simply by willing, it makes the small gland to which it is closely united move in the way requisite for producing the effect aimed at in the volition.[3]

And the others saw their task as being to make this credible – either by supposing the soul to be material (Elizabeth), by making God do the work (Malebranche, Leibniz), or by calling the mental and the material two attributes of one and the same substance (Spinoza).

Someone who has not fallen under Descartes's spell is likely to be struck by two aspects of his account of voluntary action. The first is that talk of 'volitions' does not reflect something in our everyday experience of doing things; rather, volitions are postulated, in the Cartesian theory, to serve as the mental causes of the changes in the brain which result in motions of the

[1] Anscombe and Geach (1954) p. 278.

[2] Ibid., p. 279.

[3] Smith (1952) p. 298. The gland to which Descartes refers is the pineal gland, 'the most inward of all the parts of the brain'.

body. Secondly, motions of the body, as such, are not actions. One can observe the motions of a person's body and still ask 'What is he doing?' And only someone with a philosophical theory to defend would say that the answer to 'What is he doing?' – e.g. 'He's dancing', 'He's sowing seeds', 'He's baptizing a baby' – is about a mental cause of the motions of his body. Admittedly *the* way to find out what he is doing is to ask him, but one needs to understand his answer. His answer is in terms of things like dancing, sowing, and baptizing. And these are not mental events.

These are objections to Descartes's account of voluntary action that have been made, in one form or another, by a number of philosophers in recent years.[1] But Descartes's account of voluntary action is only half of his doctrine of the interaction of soul and body. There is also the action of the brain on the mind, in perception. Is the Cartesian account of perception open to objections like those to the Cartesian account of voluntary action?

THE UNIVERSAL IN PERCEPTION

VESEY I've called this talk 'The Universal in Perception' so perhaps I should begin by explaining the term 'universal'. We say 'That sunflower is tall', 'This melon is ripe', 'My boat, the Esmeralda, is blue', 'Joanna's hair is soft', and so on. We use words like 'tall', 'ripe', 'blue' and 'soft' to describe particular things. And what the things are, we indicate by using expressions like 'that sunflower', 'this melon', 'my boat Esmeralda' and 'Joanna's hair'. We might say: we have in our language some expressions, like 'that sunflower' and 'this melon', which stand for particular things, and others, like 'tall' and 'ripe' which, well, don't stand for particular things. Now, suppose someone were to say 'But surely words like "tall" and "ripe" must stand for something; after all, they aren't meaningless; so what do they stand for, if not particular things?' The tailor-made answer – or perhaps I should say philosopher-made answer – to that question is: words like 'tall' and 'ripe' stand for universals.

The idea is this. Only one thing can be that sunflower. But many things can be tall. Tallness is something that can be found anywhere in the universe. It's something that any number of things can have in common. Hence the term 'universal'. The correlative term is 'particular'. That sunflower is a particular. Tallness is a universal.

There are simple universals and complex ones. Blueness is a simple one. An example of a complex one is: being a rodent. My daughter's dormouse is a rodent. So is the squirrel that eats my walnuts. And the beaver we saw at the

[1] See, for example, Ryle (1963) Chapter 3.

zoo last week. They all have the property of being rodents. Being a rodent is something they have in common. It's a universal; but not a simple one, like blueness.

What I mean by calling being-a-rodent a complex universal, but blueness a simple one, is this. Suppose there is a porcupine in front of us, and I say 'It's a rodent', and you say 'How do you know?' I may say 'I've seen its teeth, and how it uses them. It uses them for gnawing all right. And it's got no canine teeth.' But suppose that what is in front of us is my boat, the Esmeralda. It would be absurd for me to ask you 'How do you know it's blue?' You can see it is, straight off. If your eyes are all right, that is. There's no business of giving reasons for saying it's blue, as there is for saying something's a rodent. Being blue is a simple sensory quality. Being a rodent isn't.

The next question is: What do I mean by 'the universal *in perception*'? Well, by 'perceiving', of course, I mean seeing and hearing and feeling and smelling, and so on. If someone says to me 'How do you know Joanna's hair is soft?' I may say 'I've felt it'. If they say 'How do you know my boat Esmeralda is blue?' I may say 'I've seen it'. Feeling and seeing are ways of perceiving things.

Now, my point is this. When I see something I see it as having certain qualities, characteristics – call them what you like – which it could have in common with other things. I see it as having this, that, or the other colour; this, that, or the other shape; and so on. It may be so foggy that I get only the vaguest impression of the object's qualities. But if I see it at all I must see it as something to which some description, vague or precise, is applicable on the basis of my perception of it.

Now, I can imagine you thinking: Unless I've missed something, he means no more than that when we see things we see them as having some shape, size, colour, etc., when we feel them, we feel them as being hot or cold, hard or soft, rough or smooth, etc., when we hear them we hear them as being loud or soft, high-pitched or low-pitched, etc. And so on. He calls these things 'universals'. And so he talks about 'the universal in perception'. But isn't what he means so obvious as hardly to be worth mentioning?

My answer is: That *is* all I mean. But it *is* worth mentioning. Why? Because if what I've said is true then a widely-held theory of perception – I'll call it 'the causal theory' – must be false. And my aim is to show that the causal theory *is* false. So, in fact, all this talk about 'the universal in perception' is preliminary to an attack on the causal theory in perception.

This theory is as follows:

In perception what happens is this. The physical object causes a change in the perceiver's sense-organ. This is known as 'stimulation' of the sense-organ. The stimulation causes an impulse to be passed along a nerve to the brain. This in turn causes a change in the state of the brain. This change in the state of the brain causes a sensation in the mind of the perceiver. This sensation is then interpreted in the light of past experience as being a sensation of some specific sort – such as a sensation of blueness.

The very last part of the theory – the interpretation of sensations – is necessary because causes and effects are particulars. And you have to bring in universality somehow, or else perceiving wouldn't be a way of coming to know things about the world.

Well, that's the theory. It's widely-held, and there are two good reasons for that. First, the part which it is possible to check up on, scientifically, happens to be true. Secondly, the part which it *isn't* possible to check up on scientifically has the backing of the philosophy of people like René Descartes, John Locke and John Stuart Mill. So part of it has the authority of science, and the other part has the authority of influential philosophers. The part it's possible to check up on scientifically is as follows:

> In perception what happens is this. The physical object causes a change in the perceiver's sense-organ. This is known as 'stimulation' of the sense-organ. The stimulation causes an impulse to be passed along a nerve to the brain. This in turn causes a change in the state of the brain.

With that part I have no quarrel. I've got more sense than to take on the scientists at their own game. But I do want to attack the other part. Here it is, again:

> This change in the state of the brain causes a sensation in the mind of the perceiver. This sensation is then interpreted in the light of past experience as being a sensation of some specific sort – such as a sensation of blueness.

This part of the causal theory can't be checked up on scientifically. Let me explain. First of all, the bit about a change in the state of the brain causing a sensation in the mind. The scientist is either an observer of someone perceiving something, or he's the perceiver himself. If he's an observer then with suitable electrical apparatus he can observe changes in the state of the perceiver's brain. But can he observe the brain-changes causing sensations in the perceiver's mind? What he can observe, of course, is that a certain brain-change is immediately followed by something the perceiver *does*, such as his saying 'Now it's blue'. But there is nothing in his observations to correspond to the bit about brain-changes causing sensations.

What if the scientist is himself the perceiver? Is he then in a better position to observe a brain-change causing something in his mind? No, again.

Suppose he looks at my blue boat. What he is aware of is my blue boat, not a brain-change causing a sensation. Indeed there's nothing in his experience, as the perceiver, to correspond to any part of the causal theory. So the part of the causal theory about a change in the brain causing a sensation in the mind isn't there because of what people have observed to happen in perception. It's a piece of philosophical theorizing.

All right; well, is it good philosophical theorizing, or bad? To find out, let's look at the last bit of the causal theory.

> This sensation is then interpreted in the light of past experience as being a sensation of some specific sort – such as a sensation of blueness.

Now, this is where the distinction I made between complex universals and simple ones comes in. I gave the examples that being a rodent is a complex universal; being blue is a simple one. I'm going to argue that the bit about 'interpreting in the light of past experience' makes sense in the case of complex universals, but not in the case of simple ones. And that since it doesn't make sense in the case of simple ones the non-scientific last part of the causal theory of perception is no good, incoherent.

Let's begin with a complex universal. There's something on the desk in front of me and you've got to guess what it is. If you could see it you'd see that it's white, oval, not glossy, and small enough for me to get my fingers round. It's cold. And it's not heavy. I'm going to see if I can squeeze it into a different shape. [*Sound of egg breaking*] Rather a messy experiment! It was, of course, an egg. You'd have known straight away if you'd seen it. But – and this is the point – only because of your past experience.

Now, being an egg is a complex universal. It makes sense to ask 'How do you know it's an egg?' If you couldn't see that it was white, oval, etc., you wouldn't know it was an egg.

The whiteness of the egg, on the other hand, is a simple universal.

The question is: Can what is said about a complex universal equally well be said about a simple universal? Is awareness of something as white, for instance, the result of interpretation in the light of past experience?

My own answer to this question is: No, of course not. Whiteness being a simple sensory quality there's nothing more basic to form the subject of interpretation. If you don't see the thing as having some colour straight away then all the past experience in the world won't help you to see its colour.

Now, this is where we get to the really interesting bit. The holders of the causal theory know that the last part of the theory isn't empirical. That is, they know that nothing in the experience either of someone observing the perceiver, or of the perceiver himself, corresponds to the part about changes in the brain causing sensations in the mind. It's a piece of philosophical theorizing. As such, it stands or falls with their talk of the sensations in the mind being interpreted in the light of past experience. So they can't give way on that. They must, somehow, defend the view that when something looks white to me I have interpreted a sensation.

How do they do it? Take John Stuart Mill. He tries to solve the problem with a theory about the meaning of the word 'white'. You can find it in the first book of his *System of Logic*. This is the gist of what he says:

> When we aren't doing philosophy we think of there being things, such as snowballs, which look white to us, and which we accordingly describe by using the word 'white'. But when we philosophize we realize that we can't know anything of such external objects but the particular sensations they excite in us. So the explanation of the meaning of the word 'white' must be by reference to these sensations. And the explanation is this: When I call a sensation 'a sensation of white' what I mean is that it is like a sensation I have had before, and on which I bestowed the name 'white'.
>
> Since all that anyone is directly conscious of, in perception, are the sensations excited in his mind, this is all that the word 'white' can mean to anyone.

On this view, interpreting a sensation is a matter of seeing its likeness to an earlier sensation on which a name, such as 'sensation of white' had been bestowed.

The question is: Is this a coherent theory? But before we get on to that, let me just draw your attention to one consequence of the theory. It is that what *I* mean by 'white' can't be what *you* mean. When I call a sensation 'a sensation of white' I mean it is like an earlier sensation of *mine*. When you call a sensation 'a sensation of white' you mean it is like an earlier sensation of *yours*.

Now for the question 'Is the theory coherent?' The crux of it is that I call a present sensation 'a sensation of white' because it is like an earlier sensation to which I gave the name 'white'. *My* question is: *In what respect* is the later sensation like the earlier one? And can that question be answered without using the word 'white' in a way that isn't allowed for on the theory?

On the theory we're discussing, the word 'white' is used in two ways. The first time I use it it's a proper name of a sensation, just as 'Fido' is the proper name of a dog. Subsequently, it signifies a relation – a relation of likeness between a later sensation and the earlier one. But – and this is my point – for the relation of likeness to exist the two sensations must share some quality. They must both be correctly describable as, say, white.

Let me sum that up. On the causal theory I apprehend the whiteness of a particular sensation by seeing its likeness to an earlier sensation. That is what's meant by interpreting it in the light of past experience. And my objection to that is that this talk of 'likeness' presupposes what it's supposed to explain – the use of the word 'white' to *describe* things. For if two things aren't both describable as white then they aren't both white. And if they aren't both white then they aren't like one another in that respect. Qualities are logically prior to relations of resemblance. You can't conjure qualities out of relations. Relations presuppose things to be related. So Mill's theory of the meaning of 'white' can't even be understood unless it's false.

Now let me get back to the main issue. The basic assumption of the theory I'm attacking is that there are two different things, bodies and minds, and that anything involving them both, like perception, must be explicable in terms of something in one of them *causing* something in the other. Thus, in perception it is said that there is an effect, called a sensation, in the perceiver's mind, caused by a change in the state of his brain. Now an effect is a *particular*. But knowing something about the world means being aware that something is characterized by a *universal*. So: if perceiving is coming to know something about the world it's not enough to have a sensation. Universality must be brought into the picture somehow. And it's brought in, on the theory I'm attacking, by saying that the effect, the sensation, undergoes something called 'interpretation'.

What I'm saying, on the contrary, is that the universal is in perception from the start. Or, to put it another way, perception is 'concept dependent'.

Now, to say that is to leave us with the question 'What explains our having the concepts we have?' What are we to put in the place of John Stuart Mill's empiricism as an explanation of concept-formation? But that's a topic for another talk.

GUIDE TO FURTHER READING

In the talk it is said that the part of the causal theory which it is not possible to check up on scientifically has the backing of the philosophy of René Descartes, John Locke and John Stuart Mill.

Descartes held body and mind to be two substances which interact causally. In his view perceiving involves there being something in the mind which is an *effect* of stimulation of the sense-organs. This effect is variously called a 'sense-impression', 'sensation' or 'idea'.

Locke grafted on to this a theory about the 'immediate signification' of words. He said that 'words, as they are used by man, can properly and immediately signify nothing but the ideas that are in the mind of the speaker.'[1]

---

[1] Pringle–Pattison (1924) p. 225.

If ideas are particulars, as they must be if they are effects, this leaves unexplained how there can be general words, that is, words for universals. Locke recognized the need for an account of how, as he put it, 'universals, whether ideas or terms, are made'.[1] The account he supplied was in terms of what he called 'abstraction'. We consider the ideas we get on looking at particular objects as 'separate from all other existences and the circumstances of real existence, [such] as time, place, or any other concomitant ideas'. By this act of considering them as separate, Locke says, 'ideas taken from particular beings become general representatives of all of the same kind'.

There is obviously something missing in this supposed explanation of how universals are made. It is like saying that if you physically separate one person from a group of people he automatically becomes their representative, speaking for their common interests, etc. If 'abstraction' is to explain how universals are made there must be more to it than mere separation, in thought, of a particular idea from accompanying ideas. But what?

John Stuart Mill inherited from Descartes the notion that perception is to be explained in causal terms, and therefore that it involves sensations, defined as the effects in the mind of changes in the brain produced by stimulation of the sense-organs. And he inherited from Locke the notion that words have meaning by being names. He did his best to solve the problem posed by this inheritance, the problem Locke tried to solve with 'abstraction'.

There are relevant extracts from Locke's *Essay* (Bk. II, Ch. 2, Bk. III, Chs. 2 and 3) and from Mill's *System of Logic* (Bk. I, Chs. 3, 5 and 8) in *Fundamental Problems in Philosophy*, edited by Oswald Hanfling, pp. 367–77, 397–400.

At the very end of the talk the question is asked: What are we to put in the place of John Stuart Mill's empiricism as an explanation of concept-formation? One philosopher who can be regarded as putting something in the place of Mill's empiricism is Ludwig Wittgenstein. He writes in his *Philosophical Investigations* of the formation of concepts being 'explained by facts of nature'.[2] Some help in understanding what he means by this can be obtained from reading A. R. Manser, 'Games and Family Resemblances'[3] and the Foreword to *Understanding Wittgenstein*, edited by Godfrey Vesey.[4]

[1] Ibid., p. 89.

[2] Wittgenstein (1953) Part II, Section xii.

[3] Manser (1967).

[4] Vesey (1974).

CHAPTER NINE

Interrogating Nature

HOW IS SCIENCE TO BE DISTINGUISHED FROM PSEUDOSCIENCE ?

John Stuart Mill carried his empiricism into philosophy of science. Book III of his *System of Logic* is entitled 'Of Induction'. In Chapter Three, Mill says that induction 'consists in inferring from some individual instances in which a phenomenon is observed to occur, that it occurs in all instances of a certain class, namely, in all which *resemble* the former, in what are regarded as the material circumstances.' He goes on to remark that

> there is a principle implied in the very statement of what Induction is; an assumption with regard to the course of nature and the order of the universe; namely, that there are such things in nature as parallel cases; that what happens once will, under a sufficient degree of similarity of circumstances, happen again, and not only again, but as often as the same circumstances recur.

Mill summarizes this as 'the proposition that the course of nature is uniform', and says that it is 'the fundamental principle, or general axiom, of Induction'.

On this conception of the philosophy of science, the philosopher should be establishing two things. He should be establishing 'the fundamental principle of Induction'; and he should be establishing ways of distinguishing 'material circumstances' from those that are immaterial.

This conception of the philosophy of science survived for many years despite the failure of philosophers to establish the fundamental principle they thought had to be established for science to be respectable, and despite the fact that their recipes for distinguishing material from immaterial circumstances (e.g. Mill's 'methods of experimental inquiry') bore little resemblance to the actual procedures of working scientists.

The demise of this conception of the philosophy of science is due in no small measure to the work of Sir Karl Popper.

The spiritual heirs of Hume and Mill were Ernst Mach (1836–1916) and the logical positivists of the so-called Vienna Circle. The logical positivists took the problem of distinguishing science from pseudoscience and metaphysics to be one of distinguishing meaningful from meaningless discourse, and proposed empirical verifiability as the criterion of a sentence being meaningful. What struck Popper, who was not a member of the Circle but was in close touch with its members, was that psychoanalysts habitually point to facts which, they claim, bear out their theories. Evidently verifiability, as a criterion, did not serve to rule out what Popper regarded as pseudosciences. In place of verifiability, he proposed *falsifiability* as the criterion of the scientific character of a theory. In the talk that follows this is explained thus: 'a theory is "scientific" if one is prepared to specify *in advance* a crucial experiment (or observation) which can *falsify* it, and it is pseudoscientific if one refuses to specify such a "potential falsifier".'

The following talk is by Imre Lakatos, who succeeded Sir Karl Popper as Professor of Logic and Scientific Method at the London School of Economics, University of London.

SCIENCE AND PSEUDOSCIENCE

LAKATOS Man's respect for knowledge is one of his most peculiar characteristics. Knowledge in Latin is *scientia*, and science came to be the name of the most respectable kind of knowledge. But what distinguishes knowledge from superstition, ideology or pseudoscience? The Catholic Church excommunicated Copernicans, the Communist Party persecuted Mendelians on the ground that their doctrines were pseudoscientific. The demarcation between science and pseudoscience is not merely a problem of armchair philosophy: it is of vital social and political relevance.

Many philosophers have tried to solve the problem of demarcation in the following terms: a statement constitutes knowledge if sufficiently many people believe it sufficiently strongly. But the history of thought shows us that many people were totally committed to absurd beliefs. If the strength of beliefs were a hallmark of knowledge, we should have to rank some tales about demons, angels, devils, and of heaven and hell as knowledge. Scientists, on the other hand, are very sceptical even of their best theories. Newton's is the most powerful theory science has yet produced, but Newton himself never believed that bodies attract each other at a distance. So no degree of commitment to beliefs makes them knowledge. Indeed, the hallmark of scientific behaviour is a certain scepticism even towards one's most cherished theories. Blind commitment to a theory is not an intellectual virtue: it is an intellectual crime.

Thus a statement may be pseudoscientific even if it is eminently 'plausible' and everybody believes in it, and it may be scientifically valuable even if it is unbelievable and nobody believes in it. A theory may even be of supreme scientific value even if no one understands it, let alone believes it.

The cognitive value of a theory has nothing to do with its psychological influence on people's minds. Belief, commitment, understanding are states of the human mind. But the objective, scientific value of a theory is independent of the human mind which creates it or understands it. Its scientific value depends only on what objective support these conjectures have in facts. As Hume said:

> If we take in our hand any volume; of divinity, or school metaphysics, for instance; let us ask, does it contain any abstract reasoning concerning quantity or number? No. Does it contain any experimental reasoning concerning matter of fact and existence? No. Commit it then to the flames. For it can contain nothing but sophistry and illusion.

But what is 'experimental' reasoning? If we look at the vast seventeenth-century literature on witchcraft, it is full of reports of careful observations and sworn evidence – even of experiments. Glanvill, the house philosopher of the early Royal Society, regarded witchcraft as the paradigm of experimental reasoning. We have to define experimental reasoning before we start Humean book burning.

In scientific reasoning, theories are confronted with facts; and one of the central conditions of scientific reasoning is that theories must be supported by facts. Now how exactly can facts support theory?

Several different answers have been proposed. Newton himself thought that he proved his laws from facts. He was proud of not uttering mere hypotheses: he only published theories proven from facts. In particular, he claimed that he deduced his laws from the 'phenomena' provided by Kepler. But his boast was nonsense, since according to Kepler, planets move in ellipses, but according to Newton's theory, planets would move in ellipses only if the planets did not disturb each other in their motion. But they do. This is why Newton had to devise a perturbation theory from which it follows that no planet moves in an ellipse.

One can today easily demonstrate that there can be no valid derivation of a law of nature from any finite number of facts; but we still keep reading about scientific theories being proved from facts. Why this stubborn resistance to elementary logic?

There is a very plausible explanation. Scientists want to make their theories respectable, deserving of the title 'science', that is, genuine knowledge. Now the most relevant knowledge in the seventeenth century, when science was born, concerned God, the Devil, Heaven and Hell. If one got one's conjectures about matters of divinity wrong, the consequence of one's mistake was eternal damnation. Theological knowledge cannot be fallible: it must be beyond doubt. Now the Enlightenment thought that we were fallible and ignorant about matters theological. There is no scientific theology and, therefore, no theological knowledge. Knowledge can only be about Nature, but this new type of knowledge had to be judged by the standards they took over straight from theology: it had to be proven beyond doubt. Science had to achieve the very certainty which had escaped theology. A scientist, worthy of the name, was not allowed to guess: he had to prove each sentence he uttered from facts. This was the criterion of scientific honesty. Theories unproven from facts were regarded as sinful pseudoscience, heresy in the scientific community.

It was only the downfall of Newtonian theory in this century which made scientists realize that their standards of honesty had been utopian. Before Einstein most scientists thought that Newton had deciphered God's ultimate laws by proving them from the facts. Ampère, in the early nineteenth century, felt he had to call his book on his speculations concerning electromagnetism: *Mathematical Theory of Electrodynamic Phenomena Unequivocally Deduced from Experiment.* But at the end of the volume he casually confesses that some of the experiments were never performed and even that the necessary instruments had not been constructed!

If all scientific theories are equally unprovable, what distinguishes scientific knowledge from ignorance, science from pseudoscience?

One answer to this question was provided in the twentieth century by 'inductive logicians'. Inductive logic set out to define the probabilities of different theories according to the available total evidence. If the mathematical probability of a theory is high, it qualifies as scientific; if it is low or even zero, it is not scientific. Thus the hallmark of scientific honesty would be never to say anything that is not at least highly probable. Probabilism has an attractive feature: instead of simply providing a black-and-white distinction between science and pseudoscience, it provides a continuous scale from poor theories with low probability to good theories with high probability. But, in 1934, Karl Popper, one of the most influential philosophers of our time, argued that the mathematical probability of all theories, scientific or pseudoscientific, given *any* amount of evidence is zero. If Popper is right, scientific theories are not only equally unprovable but also equally improbable. A new demarcation criterion was needed and Popper proposed a rather stunning one. A theory may be scientific even if there is not a shred of evidence in its favour, and it may be pseudoscientific even if all the available evidence is in its favour. That is, the scientific or non-scientific character of a theory can be determined independently of the facts. A theory is 'scientific' if one is pre-pared to specify in advance a crucial experiment (or observation) which can falsify it, and it is pseudoscientific if one refuses to specify such a 'potential falsifier'. But if so, we do not demarcate scientific theories from pseudo-scientific ones, but rather scientific method from non-scientific method. Marxism, for a Popperian, is scientific if the Marxists are prepared to specify facts which, if observed, make them give up Marxism. If they refuse to do so, Marxism becomes a pseudoscience. It is always interesting to ask a Marxist, what conceivable event would make him abandon his Marxism. If he is committed to Marxism, he is bound to find it immoral to specify a state of affairs which can falsify it. Thus a proposition may petrify into pseudo-scientific dogma or become genuine knowledge, depending on whether we are prepared to state observable conditions which would refute it.

Is, then, Popper's falsifiability criterion the solution to the problem of demarcating science from pseudoscience? No. For Popper's criterion ignores the remarkable tenacity of scientific theories. Scientists have thick skins. They do not abandon a theory merely because facts contradict it. They normally either invent some rescue hypothesis to explain what they then call a mere anomaly or, if they cannot explain the anomaly, they ignore it, and direct their attention to other problems. Note that scientists talk about anomalies, recalcitrant instances, not refutations. History of science, of course, is full of accounts of how crucial experiments allegedly killed theories. But such accounts are fabricated long after the theory had been abandoned. Had Popper ever asked a Newtonian scientist under what experimental conditions he would abandon Newtonian theory, some Newtonian scientists would have been exactly as nonplussed as are some Marxists.

What, then, is the hallmark of science? Do we have to capitulate and agree that a scientific revolution is just an irrational change in commitment, that it is a religious conversion? Tom Kuhn, a distinguished American philosopher of science, arrived at this conclusion after discovering the naïvety of Popper's falsificationism. But if Kuhn is right, then there is no explicit demarcation between science and pseudoscience, no distinction between scientific progress and intellectual decay, there is no objective standard of honesty. But what criteria can he then offer to demarcate scientific progress from intellectual degeneration?

In the last few years I have been advocating a methodology of scientific research programmes, which solves some of the problems which both Popper and Kuhn failed to solve.

First, I claim that the typical descriptive unit of great scientific achieve-ments is not an isolated hypothesis but rather a research programme. Science is not simply trial-and-error, a series of conjectures and refutations. 'All swans are white' may be falsified by the discovery of one black swan. But such trivial trial and error does not rank as science. Newtonian science, for instance, is not simply a set of four conjectures – the three laws of mechanics and the law of gravitation. These four laws constitute only the 'hard core' of the Newtonian programme. But this hard core is tenaciously protected from refutation by a vast 'protective belt' of auxiliary hypotheses. And, even more importantly, the research programme has also a 'heuristic', that is, a powerful problem-solving machinery, which, with the help of sophisticated mathematical techniques, digests anomalies and even turns them into positive evidence. For instance, if a planet does not move exactly as it should, the Newtonian scientist checks his conjectures concerning atmospheric refraction, concerning propagation of light in magnetic storms, and hundreds of other conjectures which are all part of the programme. He may even invent a hitherto unknown planet and calculate its position, mass and velocity in order to explain the anomaly.

Now, Newton's theory of gravitation, Einstein's relativity theory, quantum mechanics, Marxism, Freudism, are all research programmes, each with a characteristic hard core stubbornly defended, each with its more flexible protective belt and each with its elaborate problem-solving machinery. Each of them, at any stage of its development, has unsolved problems and undigested anomalies. All theories, in this sense, are born refuted and die refuted. But are they equally good? Until now I have been describing what research programmes are like. But how can one distinguish a scientific or progressive programme from a pseudoscientific or degenerating one?

Contrary to Popper, the difference cannot be that some are still unrefuted, while others are already refuted. When Newton published his *Principia*, it was common knowledge that it could not properly explain even the motion of the moon; in fact, lunar motion refuted Newton. Kaufmann, a distinguished physicist, refuted Einstein's relativity theory in the very year it was published. But all the research programmes I admire have one characteristic in common. They all predict novel facts, facts which had been either undreamt of, or have indeed been contradicted by previous or rival programmes. In 1686, when Newton published his theory of gravitation, there were, for instance, two current theories concerning comets. The more popular one regarded comets as a signal from an angry God warning that He will strike and bring disaster. A little known theory of Kepler's held that comets were celestial bodies moving along straight lines. Now according to Newtonian theory, some of them moved in hyperbolas or parabolas never to return; others moved in ordinary ellipses. Halley, working in Newton's programme, calculated on the basis of observing a brief stretch of a comet's path that it would return in seventy-two years' time; he calculated to the minute when it would be seen again at a well-defined point of the sky. This was incredible. But seventy-two years later, when both Newton and Halley were long dead, Halley's comet returned exactly as Halley predicted. Similarly, Newtonian scientists predicted the existence and exact motion of small planets which had never been observed before. Or let us take Einstein's programme. This programme made the stunning prediction that if one measures the distance between two stars in the night and if one measures the distance between them during the day (when they are visible during an eclipse of the sun), the two measurements will be different. Nobody had thought to make such an observation before Einstein's programme. Thus in a progressive research programme theory leads to the discovery of hitherto unknown novel facts. In degenerating programmes, however, theories are fabricated only in order to accommodate known facts. Has, for instance, Marxism ever predicted a stunning novel fact successfully? Never! It has some famous unsuccessful predictions. It predicted the absolute impoverishment of the working class. It predicted that the first socialist revolution would take place in the industrially most developed society. It predicted that socialist societies would be free of revolutions. It predicted that there will be no conflict of interests between socialist countries. Thus the early predictions of Marxism were bold and stunning but they failed. Marxists explained all their failures: they explained the rising living standards of the working class by devising a theory of imperialism; they even explained why the first socialist revolution occurred in industrially backward Russia. They 'explained' Berlin 1953, Budapest 1956, Prague 1968. They 'explained' the Russian–Chinese conflict. But their auxiliary hypotheses were all cooked up after the event to protect Marxian theory from the facts. The Newtonian programme led to novel facts; the Marxian lagged behind the facts and has been running fast to catch up with them.

To sum up. The hallmark of empirical progress is not trivial verifications: Popper is right that there are millions of them. It is no success for Newtonian theory that stones, when dropped, fall towards the earth, no matter how often this is repeated. But so-called 'refutations' are not the hallmark of empirical failure, as Popper has preached, since all programmes grow in a permanent ocean of anomalies. What really count are dramatic, unexpected, stunning predictions: a few of them are enough to tilt the balance; where theory lags behind the facts, we are dealing with miserable degenerating research programmes.

Now, how do scientific revolutions come about? If we have two rival research programmes, and one is progressing while the other is degenerating, scientists tend to join the progressive programme. This is the rationale of scientific revolutions. But while it is a matter of intellectual honesty to keep the record public, it is not dishonest to stick to a degenerating programme and try to turn it into a progressive one.

As opposed to Popper the methodology of scientific research programmes does not offer instant rationality. One must treat budding programmes leniently: programmes may take decades before they get off the ground and become empirically progressive. Criticism is not a Popperian quick kill, by refutation. Important criticism is always constructive: there is no refutation without a better theory. Kuhn is wrong in thinking that scientific revolutions are sudden, irrational changes in vision. The history of science refutes both Popper and Kuhn: on close inspection both Popperian crucial experiments and Kuhnian revolutions turn out to be myths: what normally happens is that progressive research programmes replace degenerating ones.

The problem of demarcation between science and pseudoscience has grave implications also for the institutionalization of criticism. Copernicus's theory was banned by the Catholic Church in 1616 because it was said to be pseudo-scientific. It was taken off the index in 1820 because by that time the Church deemed that facts had proved it and therefore it became scientific. The Central Committee of the Soviet Communist Party in 1949 declared Mendelian genetics pseudoscientific and had its advocates, like Academician Vavilov, killed in concentration camps; after Vavilov's murder Mendelian genetics was rehabilitated; but the Party's right to decide what is science and publishable and what is pseudoscience and punishable was upheld. The new liberal Establishment of the West also exercises the right to deny freedom of speech to what it regards as pseudoscience, as we have seen in the case of the debate concerning race and intelligence. All these judgements were inevitably based on some sort of demarcation criterion. This is why the problem of demarcation between science and pseudoscience is not a pseudo-problem of armchair philosophers: it has grave ethical and political implications.

GUIDE TO FURTHER READING

Sir Karl Popper's views on the problem of demarcating science from pseudo-science were published in his book *The Logic of Scientific Discovery*. An excellent short introduction to his philosophy of science is provided in his paper 'Science: Conjectures and Refutations' in his book *Conjectures and Refutations*.

The theories of Thomas S. Kuhn may be found in his book, *The Structure of Scientific Revolutions*.

Professor Lakatos has expounded his own theories in a number of papers. One of them, entitled 'Falsification and the Methodology of Scientific Research Programmes', followed by comments on it by T. S. Kuhn and P. K. Feyerabend, is in *Criticism and the Growth of Knowledge*, edited by I. Lakatos and A. E. Musgrave.

CHAPTER TEN

'Don't Ask for the Meaning'

WHAT IS THE MEANING OF A WORD ?

Wittgenstein's *Blue Book* begins with the question 'What is the meaning of a word?'

The first thing to notice about this question is that it is an unusual one. The usual question is, for example, 'What is the meaning of the word "abacist"?' We know how to answer the usual question. We look up the word 'abacist' in the dictionary, and find that an abacist is someone who uses an abacus in doing accounts. But the question 'What is the meaning of a word?' cannot be answered like that. (It is not the same as the question 'What is the meaning of the word "word"?')

One way of coming to see the meaning of 'What is the meaning of a word?' is to put it side by side with 'What is the meaning of a natural sign?' This, again, is an unusual question. The usual one is, for example, 'What do red skies at night mean?' By putting the two unusual questions side by side we can see the point of asking either of them. 'What is the meaning of a word?' becomes 'What is linguistic meaning as distinct from, say, natural sign meaning?' or 'What is it for certain marks or sounds to be what we call "words"?'

When the question is put like that then answers occur to us that do not occur if the question is left in the form 'What is the meaning of a word?' For instance, it is then possible to say: 'There's no *one* answer. "Fire", "sorry", "five", "red", "John", "and" and "are" are all words. But they aren't the same sort of word. Only one of them is a name, for instance. Words are used in different ways, ways which can be compared and contrasted, in rather the same way as we can compare and contrast the members of a family.'

If the question is left in the form 'What is the meaning of a word?' then it is awfully easy to forget what we know very well about the different ways words are used, and to look for an answer that would be true only if all words were used in the same way, namely 'to stand for something'.

As we have seen in the case of 'volitions' and 'sensations', philosophers have a way of finding (some would say 'inventing'!) what they are looking for. But in the case of 'what words stand for' the situation is complicated by the fact that some philosophers 'find' what-words-stand-for in their minds; others, in the world outside their minds.

The latter notion is probably the more popular, and carries with it the idea that we learn the meaning of a word by noticing that the use of it by others is associated with the presence of something which, we guess, is what the word stands for. In brief, words are learnt by 'ostensive definition'.

The other notion is exemplified in Locke:

> Man . . . had by nature his organs so fashioned as to be fit to frame articulate sounds, which we call words. But this was not enough to produce language. It was farther necessary, that he should be able to use these sounds as signs of internal conceptions; and to make them stand as marks for the ideas within his own mind, whereby they might be made known to others.[1]

It is easy not to see the full significance of this short passage. The 'internal conceptions' are not merely 'internal' as opposed to 'external'; they are also 'conceptions' ('ideas') as opposed to 'signs' (words). The point is that, according to Locke, there are not merely things one says out loud and things one keeps to oneself; there are also 'ideas', for which both the things one says out loud and the things one keeps to oneself stand, and in virtue of standing for which the spoken or unspoken things are language. This point comes out more clearly in what Locke says about mental and verbal propositions:

> We must, I say, observe two sorts of propositions that we are capable of making: First, *Mental*, wherein the ideas in our understandings are, without the use of words, put together or separated by the mind. . . . Secondly, *Verbal* propositions, which are words, the signs of our ideas, put together or separated in affirmative or negative sentences.[2]

Locke also says, about mental and verbal propositions, that

> it is very difficult to treat of them asunder. Because it is unavoidable, in treating of mental propositions, to make use of words; and then the instances of mental propositions cease immediately to be barely mental, and become verbal. And that which makes it yet harder to treat of mental and verbal propositions separately, is, that most men, if not all, in their thinking and reasonings within themselves, make use of words instead of ideas . . .[3]

[1] Pringle–Pattison (1924) p. 223.

[2] Ibid., p. 293.

[3] Ibid., pp. 291–2.

A different explanation is suggested by J. M. Cameron:

> No one when challenged is prepared to say that he is acquainted with anything at all corresponding to Locke's story [about 'mental propositions']. It *must* be like that, we sometimes hear; never, I think, Yes, that's how it is. The 'must' is here significant. It suggests that we are not being given an introspective account, but an account of what is held to follow logically from our talking about propositions as expressing thoughts. . . . Locke's argument gets its apparent force from its seeming to be a description of what goes on when we introspect; but it is a pseudo-description – not a *misdescription* of what goes on, but rather what we take to be a description but isn't so.[1]

This is where we get if we leave the question with which we began in the form 'What is the meaning of a word?' One alternative, we have seen, is to reformulate it so that it is answerable in terms of the different ways words are used. Wittgenstein embraced this alternative. His answer to 'What is the meaning of a word?' can be summed up in the aphorism 'Don't ask for the meaning, ask for the use.'

The dialogue that follows is introduced by Oswald Hanfling. The script of the dialogue is taken almost word for word from Wittgenstein's *Philosophical Investigations*, Part I, and *Zettel*. The references in square brackets are to the numbered paragraphs of these works. References to the numbered paragraphs of *Zettel* are preceded by the letter Z. References to Part I of the *Philosophical Investigations* are preceded by the letters *P.I.* The division of the material between the two speakers, A and B, is explained in Hanfling's introduction.

'DON'T ASK FOR THE MEANING, ASK FOR THE USE'

HANFLING To make an adaptation of Wittgenstein's *Philosophical Investigations* is a chancy thing to do. What he has to say is so much bound up with the way in which he says it that any adaptation must run the risk of some distortion. Fortunately I've been able, in making my adaptation, to benefit from the advice of Professor Elizabeth Anscombe, who is the translator of the *Investigations* from the German – and also, of course, from that translation itself.

One or two of the passages I have used are taken, not from the *Investigations*, but from another work of Wittgenstein's published under the title *Zettel*.

For a time I wondered whether to conceive the programme as a dialogue or

[1] Cameron (1962) pp. 127–8.

as a monologue, with the philosopher talking to himself, as it were. The book doesn't fall squarely into one or the other category. In this respect, as in several others, Wittgenstein's way of writing philosophy was, quite literally, unique.

On reflection we judged it best to present the adaptation as a discussion between two philosophers, with the parts being taken by myself and a colleague. It would be a mistake, however, to suppose that there are two clearly demarcated characters, such as you would get in a more conventional philosophical dialogue, one of whom represents the writer's own view and the other that of an imaginary opponent. With Wittgenstein the situation is more subtle, more interesting – and more difficult. Some of the time he is, pretty obviously, refuting the views of an imaginary opponent. But at other times it would be more true to regard both of the speakers as being Wittgenstein himself – Wittgenstein wrestling with his own ideas, and presenting the various facets of a problem in a multitude of different, but always highly characteristic, ways.

That's all I'm going to say by way of introduction. For the rest of the programme we shall be speaking Wittgenstein's thoughts. We begin with a quotation from the fifth-century thinker St Augustine, which gives an account of how a child learns the use of language. It's with this quotation that Wittgenstein himself opens his *Philosophical Investigations*.

B 'When my elders named some object, and accordingly moved towards some thing, I saw this and I grasped that the thing was called by the sound they uttered when they meant to point it out. Their intention was shewn by their bodily movements, as it were the natural language of all peoples: the expression of the face, the play of the eyes, the movement of other parts of the body, and the tone of voice which expresses our state of mind in seeking, having, rejecting, or avoiding something. Thus, as I heard words repeatedly used in their proper places in various sentences, I gradually learnt to understand what objects they signified; and after I had trained my mouth to form these signs, I used them to express my own desires.'

A These words, it seems to me, give us a particular picture of the essence of human language. It is this: the words of the language name objects – sentences are combinations of such names. In this picture of language we find the roots of the following idea: every word has a meaning. This meaning is correlated with the word. It is the object for which the word stands.

Now think of the following use of language: I send someone shopping. I give him a slip marked 'five red apples'. He takes the slip to the shopkeeper, who opens the drawer marked 'apples'; then he looks up the word 'red' in a table and finds a colour sample against it; then he says the series of cardinal numbers up to the word 'five' and for each number he takes an apple of the same colour as the sample out of the drawer. It is in this and similar ways that one operates with words.

B But how does he know where and how he is to look up the word 'red' and what he is to do with the word 'five'?

A Well, I assume that he *acts* as I have described. Explanations come to an end somewhere.

B Yes. . . . But what is the meaning of the word 'five'?

A No such thing was in question here, only how the word 'five' is used. [*P.I.* 1]

B But what do the words of this language signify?

A What is supposed to show what they signify, if not the kind of use they have? And that we have already described. [*P.I.*10]
    Think of the tools in a tool-box: there is a hammer, pliers, a saw, a screw-driver, a ruler, a glue-pot, glue, nails and screws. Now the functions of words are as diverse as the functions of these objects. (And in both cases there are similarities.)
    Of course, what confuses us is the uniform appearance of words when we hear them spoken or meet them in script and print. Because their *application* is not presented to us so clearly. [*P.I.* 11]
    It is like looking into the cabin of a locomotive. We see handles all looking more or less alike. (Naturally, since they are all supposed to be handled.) But one is the handle of a crank which can be moved continuously (it regulates the opening of a valve); another is the handle of a switch, which has only two effective positions, it is either on or off; a third is the handle of a brake-lever, the harder you pull on it, the harder it brakes; a fourth, the handle of a pump: it has an effect only so long as it is moved to and fro. [*P.I.* 12]

B But surely every word in language signifies something.

A In saying that we have so far said *nothing whatever*; unless we have explained exactly what distinction we wish to make. It might be, perhaps, that we wanted to distinguish the words of language from words – as we say – 'without meaning' such as occur in the poems of Lewis Carroll. [*P.I.* 13]

One thinks that learning language consists in giving names to objects. [*P.I.* 26]

Now one *can* define the name of a colour, the name of a material, a numeral and so on, ostensively. I mean, if one defines the number two by saying 'That is called "two"' while pointing to two nuts, then that's perfectly exact, isn't it?

B Hm – but how can two be defined like that? The person to whom you're giving the definition doesn't know *what* you want to call 'two'; he will suppose that 'two' is the name given to this group of nuts!

A Yes, he *may* suppose this; but perhaps he doesn't. And then again, he might make the opposite mistake; when I want to assign a name to this group of nuts, he might understand it as a numeral. In other words: an ostensive definition can in *every* case be variously interpreted. [*P.I.* 28]

B Perhaps one could say: two can only be ostensively defined in the following way: 'This *number* is called "two"'. The word 'number' here shows what place in language, in grammar, we assign to the word 'two'.

A Yes, but this means that the word 'number' must be explained before the ostensive definition can be understood. The word 'number' in the definition does indeed show the place, show the post at which we station the word 'two'. [*P.I.* 29]

So one might say: the ostensive definition explains the use – the meaning – of the word when the overall role of the word in language is already clear. One has already to know (or be able to do) something in order to be able to ask for a thing's name. [*P.I.* 30]

B But someone coming into a strange country will sometimes learn the language of the inhabitants from ostensive definitions that they give him; and he will often have to *guess* the meaning of these definitions; and will guess sometimes right, sometimes wrong.

A Yes, and now, I think, we can say: Augustine describes the learning of human language as if the child came into a strange country and didn't understand the language of the country; that is, as if it already had a language, only not this one. Or again: as if the child could already *think*, but not yet speak. And 'think' would here mean something like 'talk to itself'. [*P.I.* 32]

B But surely it's not true that you must already be master of a language in order to understand an ostensive definition: all you need is – obviously – to

know or guess what the person giving the explanation is pointing to·
Whether for example to the shape of the object, or to its colour, or to its
number, and so on.

A And what does 'pointing to the shape', 'pointing to the colour' consist in?
Point to a piece of paper. And now point to its shape, now to its colour –
now to its number (that sounds queer). How did you do it?

B I should say I *meant* a different thing each time I pointed.

A And if I ask how that is done?

B Well, I *concentrated my attention* on the colour, the shape, and so on.

A But now I ask again: how is *that* done? Look, suppose someone points to a
vase and says 'Look at that marvellous blue – ignore the shape'. Or again:
'Look at the marvellous shape – the colour doesn't matter'. No doubt you
will do something *different* when you follow these two requests.

B That's right. And don't I always do the *same* thing when I direct my
attention to the colour?

A Well . . . you sometimes *attend to* the colour by putting your hand up to
keep the outline out of sight; or by not looking at the outline of the thing;
sometimes by staring at the object and trying to remember where you saw
that colour before.
   You *attend to* the shape, sometimes by tracing it, sometimes by screwing
up your eyes so as not to see the colour clearly, and in many other ways.

B Well?

A I want to say: This is the sort of thing that happens *while* one 'directs one's
attention to this or that'. But it isn't this alone that makes us say someone
is attending to the shape, the colour, and so on. Just as a move in chess
doesn't consist simply in moving a piece in such-and-such a way on the
board – nor yet in one's thoughts and feelings as one makes the move: but
in the circumstances that we call 'playing a game of chess', 'solving a chess
problem', and so on. [*P.I.* 33]

B But suppose someone said: 'I always do the same thing when I attend to the
shape; my eye follows the outline and I feel a certain . . . mental process.'
[*P.I.* 34]

A Suppose I were to say 'Come here', pointing towards a person A. B, who is
standing next to him, takes a step towards me. I say 'No; A is to come'.
Will that be taken as a report about my mental processes?

B No . . . of course not. And yet, couldn't inferences be made from it about processes going on in you when you spoke the words 'Come here'?

A But what kind of processes?

B Mightn't it be supposed that you . . . looked at A as you gave the order? That your 'train of thoughts' led you towards him?

A But perhaps I don't know B at all; I am in touch only with A. In that case someone who guessed at my mental processes might have been quite wrong; but all the same he would have understood that I meant A and not B. [Z. 21]
  Or again, suppose I point with my hand and say 'Come here'. A asks 'Did you mean me?' I say 'No I meant B'. Now what went on when I 'meant' B (since my pointing left it in doubt which one I meant)? Well, I said those words, made that gesture. Must something further have taken place, in order for that language-use to go on? [Z. 22]

B It seems to me that you take the easy way out. You talk about all sorts of language-uses, but you've nowhere said what the essence of language is: what is common to all these activities, and what makes them into language or parts of language.

A Yes, that's true. Instead of producing something that's common to all that we call language, I am saying that these phenomena have no one thing in common which makes us use the same word for all, but that they are *related* to one another in many different ways. And it is because of this relationship, or these relationships, that we call them all 'language'. I will try to explain this. [P.I. 65]
  Consider for example the proceedings that we call 'games'. I mean board games, card games, ball games, Olympic games, and so on. What is common to them all?

B There must be something common to them all or they wouldn't . . .

A Don't say 'there *must* be something common, or they wouldn't be called "games"' – but *look and see* whether there is. If you look at them you will not see something that is common to *all*, but similarities, relationships, and a whole series of them at that. As I said: don't think but look! Look for example at board games, with their multifarious relationships. Now pass to card games. Here you find many correspondences with the first group, but many common features drop out, and others appear. When we pass to ball games, much that is common is retained, but much is lost. Are they all 'amusing'? Compare chess with noughts and crosses. Or is there always winning and losing, or competition between players? Think of patience.

In ball games there is winning and losing; but when a child throws his ball at the wall and catches it again, this feature has disappeared. Now think of games like ring-a-ring-a-roses; here is the element of amusement, but how many other characteristics have disappeared! And we can go through many, many other groups of games in the same way; and can see how similarities crop up and disappear. [*P.I.* 66]

I can think of no better expression to characterize these similarities than 'family resemblances'; for the various resemblances between members of a family: build, features, colour of eyes, gait, temperament, and so on, overlap and criss-cross in the same way. And I shall say: 'games' form a family. [*P.I.* 67]

B But then how is the concept of a game bounded? What still counts as a game and what no longer does? Can you give the boundary?

A No. You can *draw* one; for none has so far been drawn. But that never troubled you before when you used the word 'game'. [*P.I.* 68]

B But then the use of the word is unregulated. How then should we explain to someone what a game is?

A Oh, I should imagine we should describe some games to him, and we might add: 'These *and similar things* are called "games"'. And do we know any more about it ourselves? [*P.I.* 69]

B But doesn't our understanding reach beyond all examples? [*Z.* 09]

Do you really explain to the other person what you yourself understand? Don't you get him to *guess* the essential thing? You give him examples, but he has to guess their drift, to guess your intention.

A Every explanation I can give to myself I can also give to him. [*Z.* 10]

It seems to me that here we come up against a remarkable and characteristic phenomenon in philosophical investigation. The difficulty, I might say, is not to find the solution, but to recognize as the solution something that looks as if it were merely a preliminary to it. This is connected, I think, with our wrongly expecting an explanation; whereas the solution of the difficulty is a description – if, that is, we give it the right place in our considerations. If we dwell upon it, and don't try to get beyond it. The difficulty here is: to stop. [*Z.* 314]

GUIDE TO FURTHER READING

I recommend paragraphs 1–43 of Part I of Ludwig Wittgenstein, *Philosophical Investigations*, and the Preface and pages 1–44 of Ludwig Wittgenstein, *The Blue and Brown Books*.

A valuable collection of papers on meaning, including a number in which there is discussion of Wittgenstein's views, is *The Theory of Meaning*, edited by G. H. R. Parkinson. In this collection you may find the papers by Gilbert Ryle and J. N. Findlay, on 'Use, Usage and Meaning', of particular interest.

CHAPTER ELEVEN

Must God Exist?

IS THERE A RATIONAL JUSTIFICATION OF BELIEF IN GOD ?

In this chapter and the next we shall consider two related questions: (a) Can religious belief be justified rationally, by proving that God exists? (b) Is it reasonable to demand a justification of religious belief? (The questions are related in that the answer to question (b) has a bearing on the importance we should attach to a negative answer to question (a).)

Philosophers have advanced many arguments to justify belief in the existence of God. Two of the most common are known as 'the teleological argument' and 'the cosmological argument'. The teleological argument or 'argument from design', is based on the fact that, like things that have been created by man, many things in nature are well adapted for a particular end. The conclusion is that they are the product of an intelligent designer, and one who far surpasses man in his creative ability.

The cosmological argument, as its name implies, is one that involves the idea of the cosmos, that is, the idea of the world as a totality of all phenomena in space and time. The argument may take a number of forms, one of which is known as 'the argument from contingency'. This form of the argument starts out from the idea that all the things in the world are only 'contingent' in their existence. That is, whether any particular thing exists or not depends on whether something else exists. For example, I would not exist had not my mother and father existed. In other words, it is not true of any particular thing in the world that it contains *within itself* the reason for its existence.

Those who accept the argument from contingency hold that we must, in the long run, have recourse to some non-contingent, or 'necessary', being if we are to explain the existence of contingent things. There must be something that contains within itself the reason for its existence if the existence of contingent things is to have an explanation. And such a necessary being is what we mean by 'God'.

The debate that follows is an edited part of a programme that was first broadcast by the BBC in 1948. The two people taking part are Frederick Copleston, a noted Jesuit historian of philosophy, and Bertrand Russell, the eminent philosopher, logician and social reformer, who died in 1970. Russell's position, in the debate, is that of an agnostic. Copleston's is that of a believer who holds that the existence of God can be proved.

Copleston starts the discussion by stating the argument from contingency in the form in which he himself favours it.

A DEBATE ON THE EXISTENCE OF GOD

COPLESTON Suppose that I give a brief statement and that then we go on to discuss it? . . . Well, for clarity's sake I will divide the argument into distinct stages. First of all, I should say, we know that there are at least some beings in the world which do not contain in themselves the reason for their existence. For example, I depend on my parents, and now on the air, and on food, and so on. Now, secondly, the world is simply the real or imagined totality or aggregate of individual objects, none of which contain in themselves alone the reason for their existence. There isn't any world distinct from the objects which form it, any more than the human race is something apart from the members. Therefore, I should say, since objects or events exist, and since no object of experience contains within itself the reason of its existence, this totality of objects must have a reason external to itself. That reason must be an existent being. Well this being is either itself the reason for its own existence, or it is not. If it is, well and good. If not, then we must proceed further. But if we proceed to infinity in that sense, then there is no explanation of existence at all. So, I should say, in order to explain existence, we must come to a being which contains within itself the reason for its own existence – that is to say, which cannot not-exist.

RUSSELL This raises a great many points, and it is not altogether easy to know where to begin, but I think that perhaps in answering your argument the best point at which to begin is the question of a necessary being. The word 'necessary', I should maintain, can only be applied significantly to propositions. And, in fact, only to such as are analytic, that is to say such as it is self-contradictory to deny. I could only admit a necessary being if there were a being whose existence it is self-contradictory to deny. I should like to know whether you would accept Leibniz's division of propositions into truths of reason and truths of fact; the former, the truths of reason, being necessary.

COPLESTON I certainly should not subscribe to what seems to be Leibniz's idea of truths of reason and truths of fact, since it would appear that for him there are in the long run only analytic propositions. . . . I don't want to uphold the whole philosophy of Leibniz. I have made use of his argument from contingent to necessary being, basing the argument on the principle of sufficient reason, simply because it seems to me a brief and clear formulation of what is, in my opinion, the fundamental metaphysical argument for God's existence.

RUSSELL But, to my mind, a 'necessary proposition' has got to be analytic. I don't see what else it can mean. And analytic propositions are always complex and logically somewhat late. 'Irrational animals are animals' is an analytic proposition; but a proposition such as 'This is an animal' can never be analytic. Well, in fact, all the propositions that can be analytic are somewhat late in the build-up of propositions.

COPLESTON Take the proposition 'If there is a contingent being, then there is a necessary being'. I consider that that proposition hypothetically expressed is a necessary proposition. If you are going to call every necessary proposition an analytic proposition, then, in order to avoid a dispute in terminology, I would agree to call it analytic, though I don't consider it a tautological proposition. But the proposition is a necessary proposition only on the supposition that there is a contingent being. That there is a contingent being actually existing has to be discovered by experience, and the proposition that there is a contingent being is certainly not an analytic proposition, though I should maintain that once you know there is a contingent being, it follows of necessity that there is a necessary being.

RUSSELL The difficulty of this argument is that I don't admit the idea of a necessary being, and I don't admit that there is any particular meaning in calling other beings 'contingent'. These phrases don't for me have a significance except within a logic that I reject . . .

COPLESTON A 'contingent' being is a being which has not in itself the complete reason for its existence; that is what I mean by a contingent being. You know, as well as I do, that the existence of neither of us can be explained without reference to something or somebody outside us: our parents, for example. A 'necessary' being, on the other hand, means a being that must exist and cannot not-exist. You may say there is no such being, but you will find it hard to convince me that you do not understand the terms I am using. If you do not understand them, then how can you be entitled to say that such a being does not exist, if that is what you do say? . . .

RUSSELL Well, what you have been saying brings us back, it seems to me, to the ontological argument that there is a being whose essence involves existence, so that his existence is analytic. That seems to me to be impossible, and it raises of course the question of what one means by existence. And as to this, I think a subject named can never be significantly said to exist but only a subject described; and that existence, in fact, quite definitely is not a predicate.

COPLESTON Well, you say, I believe, that it is bad grammar, or rather bad syntax, to say, for example, 'T. S. Eliot exists'; one ought to say, for example, 'The author of *Murder in the Cathedral* exists'. Are you going to say that the proposition, 'The cause of the world exists', is without meaning? You may say that the world has no cause; but I fail to see how you can say that the proposition that the cause of the world exists is meaningless. Put it in the form of a question: 'Has the world a cause?' or 'Does a cause of the world exist?' Most people surely would understand the question, even if they don't agree about the answer.

RUSSELL Certainly the question 'Does a cause of the world exist?' is a question that has meaning. But if you say 'Yes, God is the cause of the world', you are using 'God' as a proper name; then 'God exists' will not be a statement that has meaning because it will follow that it cannot be an analytic proposition ever to say that this or that exists. For example, suppose you take as your subject the existent round-square. It would look like an analytic proposition that the existent round-square exists; but it doesn't exist.

COPLESTON No, it doesn't. Then surely you can't say it doesn't exist unless you have a conception of what existence is. As to the phrase 'existent round-square', I should say that it has no meaning at all.

RUSSELL I quite agree. Then I should say the same thing in another context in reference to a 'necessary being'.

COPLESTON Well, we seem to have arrived at an impasse. To say that a necessary being is a being that must exist and cannot not-exist has for me a definite meaning. For you it has no meaning.

RUSSELL Well, we can press the point a little, I think. A being that must exist and cannot not-exist, would surely, according to you, be a being whose essence involves existence.

COPLESTON Yes, a being the essence of which is to exist. But I should not be willing to argue the existence of God simply from the idea of his essence, because I don't think we have any clear intuition of God's essence as yet. I think we have to argue from the world of experience to God.

RUSSELL Yes, I quite see the distinction. But at the same time, for a being with sufficient knowledge it would be true to say 'Here is this being whose essence involves existence'.

COPLESTON Yes, certainly if anybody saw God, he would see that God must exist.

RUSSELL So that I mean there is a being whose essence involves existence, although we don't know that essence. We only know there is such a being.

COPLESTON Yes, I should add we don't know the essence *a priori*. It is only true *a posteriori* through our experience of the world that we come to a knowledge of the existence of that being. And then one argues the essence and existence must be identical. Because if God's essence and God's existence were not identical, then some sufficient reason for this existence would have to be found beyond God.

RUSSELL So it all turns on this question of sufficient reason, and I must say you haven't defined 'sufficient reason' in a way that I can understand. What do you mean by sufficient reason? You don't mean cause?

COPLESTON Not necessarily. Cause is a kind of sufficient reason. Only contingent being can have a cause. God is his own sufficient reason; and he is not the cause of himself. By sufficient reason in the full sense I mean an explanation adequate for the existence of some particular being.

RUSSELL But when is an explanation adequate? Suppose I am about to make a flame with a match. You may say that the adequate explanation of that is that I rub it on the box.

COPLESTON Well, for practical purposes; but theoretically, that is only a partial explanation. An adequate explanation must ultimately be a total explanation, to which nothing further can be added.

RUSSELL Then I can only say you are looking for something which can't be got, and which one ought not to expect to get.

COPLESTON To say that one has not found it is one thing; to say that one should not look for it seems to me rather dogmatic. What I am doing is to look for the reason, in this case the cause of the objects, the real or imaginable totality of which constitute what we call the universe. You say, I think, that the universe, or my existence, if you prefer, or any other existence, is unintelligible? . . .

RUSSELL I shouldn't say unintelligible; I think it is without explanation. Intelligibility to my mind is a different thing; intelligibility has to do with the thing itself intrinsically and not with its relations.

COPLESTON My point is that what we call the world is intrinsically unintelligible, apart from the existence of God. You see, I can't believe that the infinity of the series of events (I mean a horizontal series, so to speak), if such an infinity could be proved, would be in the slightest degree relevant to the situation. If you add up chocolates you will get chocolates after all and not a sheep. If you add up chocolates to infinity, you presumably get an infinite number of chocolates. So if you add up contingent beings to infinity, you still get contingent beings, not a necessary being. An infinite series of contingent beings would be, to my way of thinking, as unable to cause itself as one contingent being. However, you say, I think, that it is illegitimate to raise the question of what will explain the existence of any particular object?

RUSSELL It is quite all right if you mean by explaining it, simply finding a cause for it.

COPLESTON Why stop at one particular object? Why shouldn't one raise the question of the cause of the existence of all particular objects?

RUSSELL Because I see no reason to think there is any. The whole concept of cause is one we derive from our observation of particular things. I see no reason whatsoever to suppose that the total has any cause whatsoever. . . . I can illustrate what seems to me your fallacy. Every man who exists has a mother, and it seems to me your argument is that therefore the human race must have a mother, but obviously the human race hasn't a mother; that is a different logical sphere.

COPLESTON Well, I can't really see parity. If I were saying 'every object has a phenomenal cause therefore the whole series has a phenomenal cause' there would be a parity, but I am not saying that; I am saying every object has a phenomenal cause if you insist on the infinity of the series; but the series of phenomenal causes is an insufficient explanation of the series. Therefore the series has not a phenomenal cause but a transcendent cause.

RUSSELL Well, that is always assuming that not only every particular thing in the world but the world as a whole must have a cause. For that assumption I see no ground whatever. If you give me a ground I will listen to it.

COPLESTON The series of events is either caused, or it is not caused. If it is caused, there must obviously be a cause outside the series. If it is not caused, then it is sufficient to itself, and if it is sufficient to itself it is what I call necessary. But it can't be necessary since each member is contingent, and we have agreed that the total has no reality apart from its members, therefore it can't be necessary. And I should like to observe in passing that the statement 'The world is simply there and is inexplicable' can't be got out of logical analysis. . . . I cannot see how science could be conducted on any other assumption than that of order and intelligibility in nature. The physicist presupposes, at least tacitly, that there is some sense in investigating nature and looking for the causes of events, just as the detective presupposes that there is some sense in looking for the cause of a murder. The metaphysician assumes that there is sense in looking for the reason or cause of phenomena, and, not being a Kantian, I consider that the metaphysician is as justified in his assumption as the physicist. When Sartre, for example, says that the world is gratuitous, I think that he hasn't sufficiently considered what is implied by 'gratuitous'.

RUSSELL I think there seems to me a certain unwarrantable extension here. The physicist looks for causes; that does not necessarily imply that there are causes everywhere. A man may look for gold without assuming that there is gold everywhere; if he finds gold well and good, if he doesn't he has had bad luck. The same is true when the physicists look for causes. As for Sartre, I don't profess to know what he means, and I shouldn't like to be thought to interpret him; but for my part I do think the notion of the world having an explanation is a mistake. I don't see why one should expect it to have. . . .

COPLESTON Your general point then, Lord Russell, is that it is illegitimate even to ask the question of the cause of the world?

RUSSELL Yes, that is my position.

COPLESTON If it is a question that for you has no meaning, it is of course very difficult to discuss it, isn't it?

RUSSELL Yes, it is very difficult. What do you say – shall we pass on to some other issue?

COPLESTON Yes, let us. Perhaps I might say a word about religious experience.

GUIDE TO FURTHER READING

The full text of the Russell-Copleston debate is reprinted in *The Existence of God*, edited by John Hick, and in *A Modern Introduction to Philosophy*, edited by Paul Edwards and Arthur Pap. Both these books contain other writings on the various arguments for the existence of God, and on the meaningfulness of theological statements. In the collection edited by John Hick, the writings on the cosmological arguments are from Plato, St Thomas Aquinas, Copleston and David Hume.

A clearly stated cosmological proof of God's existence is to be found in Richard Taylor's *Metaphysics*.

Stuart Brown provides a helpful discussion of the cosmological arguments advanced by Aquinas, and by Taylor, in his *Proof and the Existence of God*. The same author's *Religious Belief* illustrates the thinking behind his contribution to the discussion in the next chapter.

CHAPTER TWELVE

Wittgenstein and Religious Language

IS IT REASONABLE TO DEMAND A JUSTIFICATION OF BELIEF IN GOD ?

In *Philosophy of Language I*, Oswald Hanfling writes:

> Wittgenstein's criticism of what we may call 'the search for meanings' is twofold. He shows on one hand that the kinds of things (objects in the world, ideas in the mind) that suggest themselves as being, or providing, the meaning of words cannot possibly fill that role, and that the kind of 'demonstration' (pointing, ostensive definition, etc.) that is needed to set up the relation between word and meaning cannot possibly do the trick; and on the other hand, that the search for meanings outside language rests on a mistaken conception of language. In the *Grammatik* he points out that 'the connection between "language and reality" is made by means of verbal explanations'; and concludes that 'language remains closed in upon itself, autonomous'.[1]

The first part of the twofold criticism of 'the search for meanings' was the subject of the dialogue in Chapter Ten. Let us consider the second part, Wittgenstein's thesis that 'the search for meanings outside language rests on a mistaken conception of language'.

To understand this I think we need to distinguish between, on the one hand, questions that can be asked *within* what Wittgenstein calls a 'language game', and, on the other, ones that can be asked *about* a language game. An example may help to explain this distinction.

There is the language game which consists in our practice of saying things like 'She was miserable', 'Does it hurt?', 'They were embarrassed', and 'He lost his temper'. It might be called the 'Other Minds' language game. In it we talk about the mental states of others.

It makes sense to talk of our justifying the particular things we say in this language game. For instance, in answer to the question 'How do you know

---

[1] Hanfling (1973) p. 36.

she was miserable?' we can say 'She didn't smile for a week, and spent all her time in her bedroom'.

This would be a case of justifying a particular remark *within* the language game. Suppose, however, that the question had been 'What justifies me, in general, in using Other Minds language?' This is a question *about* the language game. It is as different from 'What justifies us in saying she was sad?' as 'What is the meaning of a word?' is from 'What is the meaning of the word "abacist"?' And just as some philosophers have tried to answer the question 'What is the meaning of a word?' so some have tried to answer the question 'What justifies me in using Other Minds language?' They have tried to answer it with, for instance, an argument from analogy, on the following lines:

I have a body as well as a mind. I have noticed that when I have certain thoughts or feelings (e.g. a feeling of pain or sadness) there is characteristic bodily behaviour (e.g. crying). I have also noticed that there are bodies like mine, and that they sometimes behave like mine. By analogy with my own case, it is reasonable to suppose that when a body that is like mine behaves like mine (i.e. cries) there is a feeling of pain or sadness associated with the behaviour, i.e. a feeling of pain in the mind of the person whose body it is.

This is a case of what Hanfling calls 'the search for meanings outside language'. He is right when he says that Wittgenstein regards it as resting on a mistaken conception of language. Having the language, we can talk of justifying particular things we say in it. But to talk of justifying the language itself is to put the cart before the horse.[1] The language is autonomous.

Now, justifying belief in other minds has always, I think, been no more than an in-group exercise for philosophers – and a pointless one at that, if Wittgenstein is right. Ordinary people do not seriously question the propriety of Other Minds language. There are not missionaries, spreading the good news that there are other minds. But there *are* missionaries spreading other good news – about God and the forgiveness of sins. And there is the feeling that justifying belief in God is something to be taken seriously. Is this feeling wrong? Is religious language on a par with Other Minds language? Is it unreasonable to demand from a religious person 'a justification for his belief in miracles, holiness, the forgiveness of sins'?

These are among the questions that are raised in the following discussion between Oswald Hanfling and Stuart Brown, Senior Lecturer in Philosophy at The Open University.

---

[1] Wittgenstein (1967) § 542. See also my paper, 'Other Minds' in Vesey (1974) pp. 149–61

WITTGENSTEIN AND RELIGIOUS LANGUAGE

BROWN A man who professes a religion will hold various beliefs. This will involve him in holding that certain general terms have application to particular cases. He may hold, for example, that particular *actions* can be sinful or in accordance with the will of God, particular *events* can be miraculous, particular *places* or *objects* holy or profane, particular *people* can be saints, prophets, witches; and so on. A man who professes no religion, on the other hand, will not allow that such general terms do actually apply to anything – at least in the senses intended by believers. Characteristically, indeed, he will not use such language at all. Oscar Wilde, when he was accused of blasphemy, retorted that 'blasphemy' was a word he never used. And he did not, of course, mean that he talked instead of 'taking the Lord's name in vain' or something of that sort. Rather, it can be said, these ideas played no part in his thought or in how he understood his own actions.

In a curious way, then, believer and unbeliever seem to diverge not only in their belief but in their language. Nor is this divergence with respect to language a matter simply of preferring one terminology to another. I prefer not to use the word 'don' and prefer not to be called a 'don'. Yet I know perfectly well what others mean when they use the word and my eyes light up greedily when I read the headline 'Dons get pay rise'. The unbeliever, on the other hand, may not be sure he even understands what sort of offence against God blasphemy is supposed to be.

In this way, I think, one reaches a point at which wanting a justification for religious *belief* is no different from wanting to be shown a foundation for religious *language*. Now, one of the issues I raise in the correspondence material on *Religious Belief* concerns whether it is right to demand a general justification of religious belief. And Oswald Hanfling, in his material on the Philosophy of Language, expounds a view of the later Wittgenstein to the effect that language in general is not founded on any extra-linguistic reality and that it is wrong to demand that such a foundation be provided for it. This thesis of Wittgenstein might appear to have implications for religious language, in the following way: *If* what Wittgenstein said about language in general is true, and if what is true about language in general is true also of religious language, then religious language has no foundation and it is wrong to demand a justification for it. And if this is true, it has the very interesting and controversial consequence that it is not reasonable to demand from a religious person a justification or his belief in miracles, holiness, the forgiveness of sins, or whatever.

Since we're going to discuss whether Wittgenstein's view of language has this consequence we ought to consider first what that view is. So perhaps I can ask you, first of all, what you take Wittgenstein to have meant by saying that language in general has no foundation?

HANFLING I think perhaps the best way to approach that is by considering the view that Wittgenstein was opposed to. This is the view that I expound in the correspondence material by means of a quotation from Schlick. Schlick, you remember, observed that if you looked up a word in a dictionary you would see it defined in terms of other words; and if you looked up those words, you would again find definitions given by means of words – obviously. Now Schlick was very troubled about this. He thought that at some stage there must be a way of defining the words, and justifying their existence, by appealing to a reality *outside* language, a reality which was to be contrasted with language. And it's precisely this conception that Wittgenstein rejects when he talks about language being 'autonomous' – a kind of law to itself. He shows in a variety of ways that what we do in language *can't* be justified by pointing to something outside language. To take just one of these ways: he considers the case of someone calling an object 'red', and being asked what 'made him' call it red, what justified his use of the word. Well, in a normal case the question wouldn't make sense. The person could only say 'It jolly well is red', or 'Can't you see?' or 'I speak English', or something like that. Many philosophers have thought that there was something you could do, or demonstrate, by way of justifying the way in which language is ordinarily used. But Wittgenstein showed, on the one hand, that language didn't need this kind of foundation, and on the other, that any such demonstration, pointing or whatever, would only mean something if it were already understood *in a linguistic way*. Therefore it wasn't something 'beyond' or 'behind' language. And so language is 'autonomous' in this sense: that though you can show some uses of language to be dependent on other uses, it's a mistake to think of language *in general* as either having or needing an extra-linguistic foundation.

BROWN Sometimes, when Wittgenstein is making this sort of point he expresses it by saying that language is founded on convention. What do you think he means by this?

HANFLING Yes, he also uses the word 'arbitrary'. But I think one has to be careful here. He certainly isn't saying that at some stage people sat down and made a convention, or came to an agreement, to use ordinary language in the way we do. Nor is he saying that it's open to us to choose and change our basic concepts by making a *new* convention. And again, when he says *'founded* on convention', he doesn't mean, contrary to what I said before, that there is after all something outside language – namely a convention – which provides an independent foundation for what we do *in* language. The position is rather that the convention, or agreement, that is meant here, *is* just the fact that we all use words – ordinary words like 'red' and 'green', 'wet' and 'cold' and so on – in the same kind of way. Without such agreement, language wouldn't exist. But what is meant by autonomy, convention, and the like, is that the agreement is an agreement *in* the way we use language, and not something beyond or behind language.

BROWN That's an interesting point, but perhaps we should leave these questions and turn now to asking what implications, if any, Wittgenstein's views about language in general have for religious language. Wittgenstein did, in fact, give a few lectures on religious belief and notes from these have now been published. But his influence on the philosophy of religion is largely due not to his expressed remarks on religious belief, but to the apparent consequences of his views about language in general for religious language. For instance, he remarked in *Philosophical Investigations*, Part I, §355, that the language of sense impressions, *'like any other*, is founded on convention'. And this certainly looks like an invitation to construe every area of language as 'autonomous' and as not therefore answerable to any extra-linguistic reality. And if this is so, it follows that the language of religion is autonomous in the sense you have explained. And I think you, Ossie, want to accept the general view of language as *not* being founded upon an extra-linguistic reality, but you don't want to accept that it follows from this that sceptical attacks on religion are out of place.

HANFLING No, I don't. Of course, I don't want to say that what Wittgenstein says about autonomy is less true of religious language than of other kinds of language. But I'd like to make a distinction here between what we might call 'simple' and 'complex' terms. Let's take 'red' as an example of a simple term. Now, red is simple in the sense that the only feature that a thing must have in order for you to call it red is just its being red. By contrast, take the word 'game'. Now, as Wittgenstein showed, it isn't possible to give an exhaustive definition of a word like 'game'. Nevertheless, there are a number of features that an activity has on account of which you call it a game. These features could be *named* and given as reasons, or as a justification, for calling something a game. Again, if someone didn't know what a game is, you could explain it to him by mentioning these features. And this sort of thing doesn't make sense with the word 'red'. There aren't any features I could name on account of which I would call something red, except just its redness.

Well now, are religious terms like the word 'game' or are they like 'red'? If one says that they are like 'red', then I think one could argue that the demand for justification is misguided. On this view the non-religious person would be someone who literally doesn't know what he is talking about. He'd be rather like a blind man – a man born blind, that is – arguing about the word 'red'. In this case religious scepticism couldn't really get a foothold. But I doubt that religious believers would want to think of their language as being like that.

BROWN I think I would agree with you that what gives the sceptic about religious language a foothold, if anything does, is the connection between that language and *non*-religious language. To the extent that religious terms can be explained in *non*-religious terms, the application of religious terms will be open to assessment in non-religious terms. For instance, on one account of the term 'miracle', a miracle involves an event which is contrary to the laws of nature – an event which, if you like, is 'naturally impossible'. Particular claims to the effect that some event is a 'miracle' could, in this use of the word, be shown to be false by an explanation of that event in terms of natural causes. Furthermore, any basis there may be for belief that no event occurs which is contrary to the laws of nature must also be a basis for scepticism about miracles in this sense of the term 'miracle'. To the extent, then, that religious terms *do* permit an explanation in terms familiar to the unbeliever, this is the way in which the sceptic might raise his doubt whether those terms do indeed apply to anything.

However, it is not obvious to me that such an explanation of religious terms is always, or even characteristically, possible. Let's take another example. One of the fundamental distinctions of religion is between the 'sacred' or 'holy', on the one hand, and the 'profane' or 'secular', on the other. I don't see how one could explain that distinction in non-religious terms. On the contrary, I should be inclined to say that someone who has no appreciation of the distinction between the sacred and the profane has not begun to understand what religion is about. Perhaps this is a distinction in the language of religion which neither has nor needs justification. If so a sceptical attack on that distinction would be out of place.

HANFLING Well, it's true, of course, that words like 'holy' and 'sacred' are difficult. And you may well be right in saying that one can't get very far in explaining them in non-religious terms. Well, I think there are two possibilities to be considered. Suppose we ask a person for his *reasons* for calling something holy. And suppose – to take the first possibility – that he can give reasons. Perhaps these would depend on the existence of God. And let's suppose again that he is able to say something, that the non-believer can understand, about what he means by 'God'. If so, then of course the sceptic is back in business. He will just deny the existence of God, and so on. On the other hand, suppose that the believer refuses to give reasons for his use of the word 'holy'. He may say, 'I can't explain these words, but I and other religious people know how to use them, and they are very important to us.' If he says this, he does have a certain autonomy. But he buys his autonomy at the price of making religious language out to be an esoteric thing, understood only by people with a special sensitivity. And I don't think this is a price he would want to pay. Because, I think, religious people want to say that their beliefs are for everyman; and that they have important implications concerning the nature of the world, and our attitudes to other people, implications that anyone who speaks English can understand – though, of course, he may not *feel* about these matters in the same way as a religious person.

BROWN I am interested that you should make that objection, for it relates to an analogy I drew in the correspondence material, *Religious Belief* – an analogy between religion and art. I suggested that there might be just the same sort of difficulty for the sceptic about the existence of objects worthy of worship as there is for the sceptic about the existence of objects worthy of aesthetic appreciation. The point of worship, it might be argued, can only be appreciated from within religion much as the point of paying attention to art works can only be seen from within art. Now we don't think it an objection to, say, classical music that it is appreciated only by those who have cultivated a special sensitivity. But you evidently think that religion would be represented for the worse if it were represented as 'esoteric' in this way.

I am not sure. I think that non-participants *do* have difficulties in understanding what is going on in religion, much as the boor has in relation to art. It is not simply a question of their staying put – so to speak – and religion being presented to them in terms they already understand. To understand the point of the distinction between the sacred and the profane, for example, the non-participant would need to acquire a participant's understanding of religion. And that would require him, in imagination at least, to become a participant. If the non-participant does not make such an imaginative effort in the direction of religion it may be because he thinks he understands it already. If then religion does not seem esoteric to him this may be because he has settled too quickly for a misunderstanding of it.

Now, you object that if religion were esoteric it would lose its relevance to human life. I agree of course that, if it is esoteric, it will not appear relevant to those who do not understand it. But an appreciation of what is sacred can make a very considerable difference to a man's life. It does not follow that it makes no difference to him simply because he cannot explain in non-religious terms what difference it makes. Nor does it follow from the fact that an outsider doesn't appreciate the difference it makes, that it wouldn't make a lot of difference if he did.

HANFLING Well, leaving aside the question of what the implications might be of describing religious language as esoteric, it seems to me in any case to be a *false* description of it. And one reason I have for saying that is that people who doubt religious beliefs are very often people who previously held them. They haven't ceased to understand what they previously understood. What has happened is simply that their attitude has changed from one of belief to one of doubt.

BROWN I think it would of course be wrong to say that people who give up religion lose, in so doing, all understanding of it. But I think their understanding is changed and in such a way as no longer to be a participant's understanding. For instance, consider a man who formerly believed in confession and absolution of sins and who has now given up the practice of religion. These practices will no longer have the meaning for him that they formerly had. If he thinks of them at all he will think of them in a different way, as perhaps a substitute for psychiatry.

HANFLING I'd certainly agree that the sceptic must enter into a participant's understanding of religion as far as he can. And this may need a considerable imaginative effort on his part, especially if he has never been a participant. I still think, though, that he can gain – or retain – a sufficient understanding for the purposes of his scepticism.

BROWN Well, I'm afraid we're going to have to leave matters there. Perhaps I can try briefly to sum up what the issues in our discussion have been. What we have been trying to do is to consider whether Wittgenstein's thesis about the autonomy of language has the implication that there is no basis for general scepticism about religious belief. What has emerged is that it is a controversial matter how religious language is to be taken. On one view, in which religious language is construed as explicable in non-religious language, we agree that it is possible to be sceptical. To the extent that this view is correct, Wittgenstein's thesis about the autonomy of language has no implication for religious language. There is, however, another account of religious language which denies that it is explicable in non-religious language. We agree in thinking that religious language, on such an account, is esoteric. Hanfling thinks, however, that it would be wrong to represent religious language as not susceptible to explanation in non-religious language. And this is something we don't agree about. But, finally, we do agree that *if* religious language is esoteric, at least some religious statements are immune from sceptical attack.

GUIDE TO FURTHER READING

Stuart Brown, in the foregoing discussion, refers to an analogy he draws in his *Religious Belief* between religion and art. See, in particular, Sections 5.3 and 5.4. In Section 5.3 he suggests that someone who was impressed by the analogy between art and religion might reason thus:

> Corresponding to the fundamental religious belief in the existence of a god there is, in art, the belief that there are objects worthy of aesthetic appreciation. In each case the belief is so embedded in a way of looking, talking and behaving that to doubt it is to question the point of that way of looking, talking and behaving. For the possibility of God's non-existence no more occurs *within* religion than the possibility of there being no works of art (in the normative sense of 'objects worthy of aesthetic appreciation') occurs *within* art. Furthermore the point of worship can no more be specified in non-religious terms than the point of attending to works of art can be specified in terms acceptable to the boor. One can only explain in religious terms why the behaviour described as 'worship' is appropriate, i.e. why thanksgiving, repentance and so on are appropriate. There is, then, a point beyond which the demand for justification becomes too radical even to make sense. And the questions 'Is there really a god?' and 'Are there really works of art?' do not have sense in the way in which 'Are there really any angels?' and 'Is Anti-art really art?' have. For these latter questions can be raised within the appropriate way of thinking and discussed in its terms. But the former questions are detached from the ways of thinking to which they purport to relate. We understand them not so much as demands for justification or as doubts to which there could be any substance but as expressions of an attitude, of a failure to see any point in what goes on in art or religion.

In the same section Brown quotes approvingly from a paper by D. Z. Phillips. Phillips' views on the philosophy of religion are to be found in D. Z. Phillips, *The Concept of Prayer*, and D. Z. Phillips, *Faith and Philosophical Enquiry*. Phillips' views in *The Concept of Prayer* are discussed in a paper 'Some Remarks on Wittgenstein's Account of Religious Belief' by W. D. Hudson, in *Talk of God*, edited by G. N. A. Vesey. The same volume contains original papers on the philosophy of religion written from a variety of philosophical standpoints, by John Hick, Paul van Buren, Paul Ricoeur,

Frederick Copleston, Charles Hartshorne, H. D. Lewis, Peter Bertocci, Ian Ramsey, Ninian Smart and John Wisdom.

W. D. Hudson is also the author of *Ludwig Wittgenstein – The Bearing of His Philosophy upon Religious Belief.*

Bibliography

Ampère, A. M. (1826) *Théorie des phénomènes électro-dynamiques, uniquement déduite de l'expérience*, Paris.

Anscombe, E. and P. T. Geach (1954) ed. and tr. *Descartes: Philosophical Writings*, London, Nelson (Indiana, Bobbs-Merrill).

Armstrong, D. M. (1962) *Bodily Sensations*, London, Routledge and Kegan Paul (New York, Humanities Press).

Armstrong, D. M. (1963) 'Vesey on Sensations of Heat' *Australasian Journal of Philosophy*, Vol. 41, pp. 359–62.

Berlin, Isaiah (1969) *Four Essays on Liberty*, Oxford University Press.

Broad, C. D. (1942) 'Features in Moore's Ethical Doctrines' in P. A. Schilpp, *The Philosophy of G. E. Moore*, Evanston, Northwestern University.

Brown, Stuart (1973a) A303 Problems of Philosophy, Units 7–8, *Proof and the Existence of God*, Milton Keynes, The Open University Press.

Brown, Stuart (1973b) A303 Problems of Philosophy, Units 31–32 *Religious Belief*, Milton Keynes, The Open University Press.

Burtt, E. A. (1932) *The Metaphysical Foundations of Modern Physical Science*, revised edition, London, Kegan Paul, Trench, Trubner & Co.

Butler, J. A. V. (1954) 'Mind and Matter. A Monist View', *Science News 34*, Harmondsworth, Penguin, pp. 95–102.

Cameron, J. M. (1962) *The Night Battle*, London, Burns and Oates.

Chisholm, R. M. (1956) ed. Johann Gottlieb Fichte, *The Vocation of Man*, New York, The Liberal Arts Press.

Cranston, Maurice (1967) *Freedom*, London, Longman.

Edwards, P. and A. Pap (1973) eds. *A Modern Introduction to Philosophy*, third edition, New York, Collier-Macmillan.

Findlay, J. N. (1949) 'God's Non-Existence', *Mind*, Vol. LVIII, pp. 352–4.

Foot, Philippa (1959) 'Moral Beliefs', *Proceedings of the Aristotelian Society*, Vol. 59, pp. 83–104.

Foot, Philippa (1967) ed. *Theories of Ethics*, Oxford University Press.

Gay, Peter (1972) *Voltaire's Politics*, New York, Random House.

Haldane, E. S. and G. T. R. Ross (1934) tr. *The Philosophical Works of Descartes*, 2 vols., Cambridge University Press (New York, Dover).

Hanfling, Oswald (1972a) ed. *Fundamental Problems in Philosophy*, Oxford, Basil Blackwell, The Open University Press.

Hanfling, Oswald (1972b) A202 The Age of Revolutions, Units 17–18 *Kant's Copernican Revolution: Moral Philosophy*, Milton Keynes, The Open University Press.

Hanfling, Oswald (1973) A303 Problems of Philosophy, Units 14–15, *Philosophy of Language I*, Milton Keynes, The Open University Press.

Hare, R. M. (1952) *The Language of Morals*, Oxford University Press.

Hare, R. M. (1963) *Freedom and Reason*, Oxford University Press.

Hare, R. M. (1972a) *Applications of Moral Philosophy*, London, Macmillan.

Hare, R. M. (1972b) *Essays on the Moral Concepts*, London, Macmillan.

Hare, R. M. (1972c) 'Rules of War and Moral Reasoning', *Philosophy and Public Affairs*, Vol. 1, No. 2, pp. 166–181.

Hare, R. M. (1973) 'Principles', *Proceedings of the Aristotelian Society*, Vol. 73, pp. 1–18

Hick, John (1964) ed. *The Existence of God*, New York, Collier-Macmillan.

Hudson, W. D. (1968) *Ludwig Wittgenstein – The Bearing of His Philosophy upon Religious Belief*, London, Lutterworth.

Kant, Immanuel (1968) *The Moral Law* tr. H. J. Paton, London, Hutchinson.

Kenny, A. (1970) tr. and ed. *Descartes: Philosophical Letters*, Oxford University Press.

Kuhn, T. S. (1963) *The Structure of Scientific Revolutions*, Chicago University Press.

Lakatos, I. and A. E. Musgrave (1970) *Criticism and the Growth of Knowledge*, Cambridge University Press.

Leibniz, G. W. (1967) *The Leibniz-Arnauld Correspondence*, ed. and tr. H. T. Mason, Manchester University Press (New York, Barnes and Noble).

MacIver, A. M. (1936) 'Is there Mind–Body Interaction?' *Proceedings of the Aristotelian Society*, Vol. 36, pp. 97–108.

Malebranche, Nicolas (1923) *Malebranche: Dialogues on Metaphysics and Religion* tr. M. Ginsberg, London, George Allen and Unwin.

Manser, A. R. (1967) 'Games and Family Resemblances', *Philosophy*, Vol. 42, pp. 210–25.

Mill, John Stuart (1893) *A System of Logic*, London, Longman (University of Toronto Press).

Moore, G. E. (1903) *Principia Ethica*, Cambridge University Press.

Motte, Andrew (1966) ed. I. Newton, *Principia*, University of California Press.

Parfit, Derek (1971) 'Personal Identity', *The Philosophical Review*, Vol. 80, pp. 3–27.

Parfit, Derek (1973) 'Later Selves and Moral Principles' in Allan Montefiore ed. *Philosophy and Personal Relations*, London, Routledge and Kegan Paul.

Parkinson, G. H. R. (1968) ed. *The Theory of Meaning*, Oxford University Press.

Pearson, Karl (1892) *The Grammar of Science*, London, A. and C. Black (Massachusetts, Peter Smith). 2nd edition 1900.

Phillips, D. Z. (1965) *The Concept of Prayer*, London, Routledge and Kegan Paul.

Phillips, D. Z. (1970) *Faith and Philosophical Enquiry*, London, Routledge and Kegan Paul.

Phillips, D. Z. and H. O. Mounce (1965) 'On Morality's having a Point', *Philosophy*, Vol. 40, pp. 308–19.

Popper, Karl R. (1963) *Conjectures and Refutations*, London, Routledge and Kegan Paul.

Popper, Karl R. (1959) *The Logic of Scientific Discovery*, London, Hutchinson, (New York, Basic Books).

Pringle-Pattison, A. S. (1924) ed. John Locke, *An Essay concerning Human Understanding*, Oxford University Press.

Rousseau, Jean-Jacques (1969) *The Social Contract*, tr. Maurice Cranston, Harmondsworth, Penguin.

Ryle, Gilbert (1963) *The Concept of Mind*, Harmondsworth, Penguin (Pennsylvania, Barnes and Noble).

Selby-Bigge, L. A. (1888) ed. David Hume, *A Treatise of Human Nature*, Oxford University Press.

Sellars, R. W. (1932) *The Philosophy of Physical Realism*, New York, The Macmillan Co.

Shklar, Judith N. (1969) *Men and Citizens: a Study of Rousseau's Social Theory*, Cambridge University Press.

Shoemaker, Sydney (1963), *Self-Knowledge and Self-Identity*, New York, Cornell University Press.

Smith, N. K. (1952) tr. *Descartes: Philosophical Writings*, London, Macmillan.

Spinoza, Baruch (1910) *Ethics*, London, Dent.

Strawson, P. F. (1964) *Individuals*, London, Methuen (Pennsylvania, Barnes and Noble).

Taylor, Richard (1963) *Metaphysics*, New York, Prentice-Hall.

Vesey, G. N. A. (1960) 'Berkeley and Sensations of Heat', *The Philosophical Review*, Vol. 69, pp. 201–10.

Vesey, G. N. A. (1963) 'Armstrong on Sensations of Heat', *Australasian Journal of Philosophy*, Vol. 41, pp. 250–4.

Vesey, G. N. A. (1964) ed. *Body and Mind*, London, George Allen and Unwin (New York, Humanities Press).

Vesey, G. N. A. (1969) ed. *Talk of God*, Royal Institute of Philosophy Lectures, Vol. 2, 1967/8, London, Macmillan (New York, St Martin's Press).

Vesey, Godfrey (1974) ed. *Understanding Wittgenstein*, Royal Institute of Philosophy Lectures, Vol. 7, 1972/3, London, Macmillan (New York, St Martin's Press).

Warnock, G. J. (1962) ed. George Berkeley, *The Principles of Human Knowledge*, London, Collins.

Williams, Bernard (1973) *Problems of the Self*, Cambridge University Press.

Wilson, Edmund (1967) *I Thought of Daisy*, London, W. H. Allan.

Wittgenstein, Ludwig (1953) *Philosophical Investigations*, tr. G. E. M. Anscombe, Oxford, Basil Blackwell (Pennsylvania, Barnes and Noble).

Wittgenstein, Ludwig (1958) *The Blue and Brown Books*, Oxford, Basil Blackwell (Pennsylvania, Barnes and Noble).

Wittgenstein, Ludwig (1966) *Lectures and Conversations on Aesthetics, Psychology and Religious Belief*, ed., Cyril Barrett, Oxford University Press (University of California Press).

Wittgenstein, Ludwig (1967) *Zettel*, ed. G. E. M. Anscombe and G. H. von Wright, Oxford, Basil Blackwell (University of California Press).

Note on Sources

1   The dialogue 'Hylas Fights Back' was written by Godfrey Vesey, Professor of
Philosophy at The Open University. The part of Philonous is based on Philonous'
lines in the first of Berkeley's *Three Dialogues between Hylas and Philonous, in
Opposition to Sceptics and Atheists*. The part of Hylas is based on G. Vesey,
'Berkeley and Sensations of Heat' (*The Philosophical Review*, LXIX, 1960, pp 201–
210). It was first broadcast in a BBC radio programme, produced by Richard
Callanan for the OU Course A303, *Problems of Philosophy*, in 1973.

2   The dialogue 'Freedom and Foreknowledge' was written by G. H. R. Parkinson,
Reader in Philosophy at Reading University, and is based mainly on *The Leibniz-
Arnauld Correspondence* (ed. and trans. H. T. Mason, with an introduction by
G. H. R. Parkinson, Manchester University Press, 1967). It was first broadcast
in a radio programme produced by Patricia Hodgson for A303 in 1973.

3   The dialogue 'Liberty' was written by Maurice Cranston, Professor of Political
Science at the London School of Economics, University of London. It was first
broadcast in a radio programme produced by Richard Callanan for A303 in
1973.

4   The discussion 'What Use Is Moral Philosophy?' between Richard M. Hare,
White's Professor of Moral Philosophy at Oxford University, and Anthony
Kenny, Fellow of Balliol College, Oxford, was produced by Patricia Hodgson
as a television programme for A303 in 1973.

5   The discussion 'Personal Identity' between Derek Parfit, Fellow of All Souls,
Oxford, and Godfrey Vesey was first broadcast in a radio programme produced
by Mary Hoskins for A303 in 1973.

6   The dialogue 'The Princess and the Philosopher' was written by Godfrey Vesey,
and adapted for radio by John Selwyn Gilbert, with research by Richard Rowson.
It was first broadcast in a programme produced by Helen Rapp for the OU
Course A100, *Humanities: A Foundation Course*, in 1971.

7   'Body and Mind: a dialogue from Malebranche' was adapted from Nicolas
Malebranche's *Metaphysical and Religious Conversations* by Oswald Hanfling,
Lecturer in Philosophy at The Open University. It was first broadcast as a radio
programme produced by Prudence Smith for A303 in 1973.

8 'The Universal in Perception' was written by Godfrey Vesey and first broadcast as a radio talk produced by Patricia Hodgson for A303 in 1973.

9 'Science and Pseudoscience', by the late Imre Lakatos, Professor of Logic at the London School of Economics, University of London, is the full text of a talk of which the radio broadcast, produced by Patricia Hodgson for A303 in 1973, was a slightly shortened version.

10 The dialogue 'Don't Ask for the Meaning, Ask for the Use' was adapted from Ludwig Wittgenstein's *Philosophical Investigations* (Blackwell) and *Zettel* (Blackwell) by Oswald Hanfling. It was first broadcast in a radio programme produced by Prudence Smith for A303 in 1973.

11 The discussion 'A Debate on the Existence of God' between Bertrand Russell and F. C. Copleston, S.J., was first broadcast by the BBC in 1948, and then re-presented for OU Course A303 in a radio programme produced by Richard Callanan in 1973.

12 The discussion 'Wittgenstein and Religious Language' between Stuart Brown, Senior Lecturer in Philosophy at The Open University, and Oswald Hanfling, Lecturer in Philosophy at The Open University, was first broadcast in a radio programme produced by Prudence Smith for A303 in 1973.

Index